Hayek's *The Constitution of Liberty*

GW00644801

Hayek's *The Constitution of Liberty*

An Account of Its Argument

EUGENE F. MILLER

The Institute of Economic Affairs

First published in Great Britain in 2010 by
The Institute of Economic Affairs
2 Lord North Street
Westminster
London SW1P 3LB
in association with Profile Books Ltd

The mission of the Institute of Economic Affairs is to improve public
understanding of the fundamental institutions of a free society, by analysing
and expounding the role of markets in solving economic and social problems.

A CIP catalogue record for this book is available from the British Library.

ISBN 978 0 255 36637 3

Many IEA publications are translated into languages other than English or
are reprinted. Permission to translate or to reprint should be sought from the
Director General at the address above.

Typeset in Stone by MacGuru Ltd
info@macguru.org.uk

Printed and bound in Great Britain by Hobbs the Printers

CONTENTS

THE AUTHOR

Dr Eugene F. Miller (1935–2010) was a professor of political science at the University of Georgia from 1967 until his retirement in 2003. He was a student in the University of Chicago's Committee on Social Thought (PhD, 1965), where he wrote a dissertation on David Hume. F. A. Hayek chaired Miller's dissertation committee, whose other members were Leo Strauss and Joseph Cropsey. Miller edited David Hume's *Essays Moral, Political and Literary* (Liberty Fund, 1985), and published articles on Hume, Strauss and Hayek. He also published on the American Founding, the nature of liberal education, the relationship between technology and politics, and the intellectual foundations of philanthropy.

FOREWORD

F. A. Hayek was awarded the Nobel Prize in Economics in 1974. The press release announcing this award recognised that 'Hayek's contributions in the field of economic theory are both profound and original', but concluded with an apparent slap at his best-known work: 'For him it is not a matter of a simple defence of a liberal system of society as may sometimes appear from the popularised versions of his thinking.'

What the Nobel Prize announcement did not make clear was that these 'popularised versions of his thinking' were written, not by some journalistic hack as one might assume, but by Hayek himself, and that these too were profound and original. *The Road to Serfdom* (1944) and *The Constitution of Liberty* (1960) each had an impact far beyond that of the standard academic treatise on economics. Historian Alan Brinkley, in *The End of Reform: New Deal Liberalism in Recession and War*, argues that Hayek 'forced into public discourse the question of the compatibility of democracy and statism'.

The influence of Hayek on Prime Minister Margaret Thatcher is legendary. In both *The Path to Power* and *The Downing Street Years* Lady Thatcher acknowledged the influence of Hayek on her view of the world. There is also evidence of his influence on her policy decisions. Once during a party policy meeting a speaker started to argue that the Conservative Party should adopt a pragmatic middle way. According to John Ranelagh in *Thatcher's People*, 'Before he had finished speaking ... the new Party Leader reached into her briefcase and took out a book. It was Friedrich von Hayek's *The Constitution of Liberty*. Interrupting, she held the book up for all of us to see. "This," she said sternly, "is what we believe," and banged Hayek down on the table.'

But *The Constitution of Liberty* is not a narrowly conceived party tract. It favours no party, except perhaps for 'the party of life, the party that favors free growth and spontaneous evolution', which Hayek evokes in his postscript. Rather, *The Constitution of Liberty* is the culmination of four decades of reflection on the nature of economic, political and social life and the possibility of a free society. As Professor Miller cogently argues and illustrates, its three parts comprise 'a careful argument that runs through the book from beginning to end'. Part I, 'The Value of Freedom', provides the philosophical foundation and justification of a free society and defence against the major contemporary opponents of such a society. In Part II, 'Freedom and the Law', Hayek provides an account of the development of the Rule of Law as the central institution of a free society. In Part III, 'Freedom in the Welfare State', Hayek examines many areas of contemporary policy concern – social security, taxation, healthcare, housing, urban planning, natural resources and education – in light of the principles developed in the earlier parts of his study.

In a footnote in his introduction, Hayek tells the reader that 'David Hume ... will be our constant companion and sage guide throughout' *The Constitution of Liberty*. Hayek holds up Hume, along with Adam Smith, Adam Ferguson and Edmund Burke, as exemplars of the 'British tradition' of liberty. More than the others whom Hayek mentions, Hume emphasised the importance of opinion as the foundation of government. In his essay 'Of the First Principles of Government', Hume wrote, 'It is therefore, on opinion only that government is founded; and this maxim extends to the most despotic and most military governments, as well as to the most free and most popular.' The importance of opinion, and the wisdom of opinion collected over time in the form of cultural traditions, is crucial to Hayek's argument for spontaneous order and the free society.

Professor Miller does not offer his account of *The Constitution of Liberty* as a substitute for reading Hayek; rather, it is designed to be a guide to the central argument of Hayek's work and therefore belongs on the bookshelf alongside Hayek. It is written at a level accessible to the novice and simultaneously substantial enough to be of value to the specialist. Miller both provides an overview of the argument of *The Constitution of Liberty* and situates that argument within the broader context of Hayek's intellectual career, so that he touches both on antecedents and later developments.

Miller made two crucial decisions about the focus of this study that are worthy of note. First, he ignores the vast secondary literature on Hayek in order to concentrate on Hayek himself. Second, Miller decided to provide as accurate and fair a reading of Hayek's text as he could and therefore largely sets aside his own evaluation of Hayek. At a number of points in his study Miller points to tensions within Hayek's argument and notes potential problems that Hayek may or may not have seen, but he does not diverge from his primary objective of providing as clear a statement of Hayek's views as he can.

Here is but one example of Miller's decision to explicate Hayek clearly and to avoid excessive criticism. Miller notes that he studied both with Hayek and Leo Strauss, the latter of whom was well known for arguing that there are crucial differences between ancient and modern thought. Hayek denies the importance of this division and traces the origins of liberalism to ancient Greece. Miller raises the questions of whether Hayek's approach does violence to the historical record or hides potential tensions within the heart of liberal thought; but rather than answering these questions himself Miller leaves their resolution to his readers.

Eugene Miller passed away shortly after revising this text. With the publication of this study Miller has left his readers with two gifts. The first is intellectual: this volume offers a finely crafted restatement of the argument of F. A. Hayek's most comprehensive work.

Miller's second gift is more elusive but in the long run perhaps of greater importance. To use appropriately an overworked and often misapplied characterisation, Miller here provides a model of what it means to be a gentleman and a scholar. In a world in which academic reputations are made by being constantly on the attack, Miller offers an example of modesty, generosity and moderation: a serious scholar taking another's argument seriously. Miller's study of *The Constitution of Liberty* sets before the reader the same challenge that Hayek does – the challenge of engaging the text, weighing the evidence for oneself, and participating at the highest level in true self-government.

I strongly commend this careful and thought-provoking study to students, teachers, academics and others who are interested in understanding *The Constitution of Liberty*.

STEVEN D. EALY

Senior Fellow, Liberty Fund, Inc.

July 2010

SUMMARY

- The core argument that runs throughout *The Constitution of Liberty* concerns freedom and its value to the individual, to society and to civilisation at large. Without freedom of action in particular, progress in these areas would be impossible.
- Modern civilisation is in crisis because the West has lost faith in the principles of liberty or freedom (interchangeable terms for Hayek). Opinion ultimately governs our actions, and Hayek will seek to reshape it through a political philosophy that restates basic principles, vindicates fundamental values, articulates a guiding 'ideal' (the Rule of Law), and clarifies standards that ought to determine policy.
- Freedom requires that the coercion of some by others in society be reduced as much as possible. One function of government is to prevent individuals from coercing other individuals, but then government itself must be prevented from using coercion improperly. In a free society, the exercise of government's coercive power is constrained and made predictable by general rules that apply equally to all individuals, including to those who make and enforce the laws. A free society is one that empowers individuals to develop and follow their own life plans. Attempts to manipulate the environment of individuals, e.g. by withholding vital information, are insidious forms of coercion.

- Freedom and responsibility cannot be separated. Responsibility means that each individual must bear the consequences of his actions. Hayek's 'individuals' are thoroughly enmeshed in social relations.

- Forgetting that man's knowledge is severely limited, modern rationalism is constantly tempted to plan and fashion the future comprehensively. Modern rationalism dates back to seventeenth-century philosophy, but later is exhibited most powerfully by socialism in its various forms. It gives rise to a destructive quest for perfection, in which inherited rules, traditions and moral values – invaluable gifts from the past – are thoughtlessly discarded. Ignorance is inevitable, unavoidable and the reality of all men, including those who occupy positions of power. Hayek is a strong critic of modern bureaucracy.

- Social order develops through spontaneous growth as well as through some measure of deliberate construction. Spontaneous growth occurs when individuals and groups with limited knowledge interact with other individuals and groups, giving rise to unplanned patterns of behaviour and institutional forms. Hayek applauds the Scottish and other British philosophers of the late eighteenth and early nineteenth centuries for recognising the importance of spontaneous growth; and he builds on their ideas to develop the theory of social evolution that underpins his philosophy of freedom. By turning to the Scots, Hayek emphatically rejects the earlier liberal theories of John Locke and his followers, which started from natural rights and from an original contract.

- Hayek rejects the idea of a 'natural' or 'factual' equality between men. At the same time, he insists that individuals have a 'dignity' that we must respect. Hayek promises 'an ultimate justification' for freedom, which must be connected somehow to this idea of individual dignity: but he leaves the matter quite unclear. He does insist strongly that the Rule of Law permits social inequalities, whose beneficial results are generally overlooked by the misguided advocates of 'social justice'.

- Hayek regards democracy as the best practicable form of government, so long as a majority of the community is committed to individual liberty, the Rule of Law and limited government. Democracy is not a primarily a way of life, but a set of procedures for organising and operating government. There are no inherent substantive ends or core beliefs that are essential to democratic rule. By conceding that the majority of a community may embrace any set of core beliefs that it chooses, Hayek is left with no basis for opposing totalitarian democracies on democratic grounds.

- Hayek applies his understanding of the evolutionary development of society in general to the growth of legal institutions and the Rule of Law. He traces this growth to England, America and Germany, but largely excludes French legal thought, which has favoured a rationalistic approach to the law which runs counter to a free society.

- The 'ideal' of the Rule of Law requires that existing laws share certain characteristics. Law must be general; it must be known and certain and apply equally to all; it must provide for an independent judiciary; it must limit the executive by legislative and judicial rules; and it must safeguard fundamental rights and civil liberties.

- Hayek does not favour passive government, but rather one that seeks many benefits for the community. Although he shares the 'strong presumption against governments actively participating in economic efforts', he nonetheless states that the 'old formulae of laissez faire or non-intervention do not provide us with an adequate criterion for distinguishing between what is and what is not admissible in a free system'. As he explains, 'it is the character rather than the volume of government activity that is important'. In economic matters, for example, an active government that assists the spontaneous forces of the market is preferable to a less active one that does the wrong things. In this regard he sees himself as following the best of the classical liberals, such as Adam Smith.

- In cases where coercion might be involved, the policy actions of government are limited by the Rule of Law. In other cases, Hayek recommends that government's policies be judged by the principle of expediency, or what best serves the community's interest.

- In the final part of *The Constitution of Liberty* Hayek examines many areas of contemporary policy concern – social security, taxation, healthcare, housing, urban planning, natural resources and education – in light of the principles developed in the earlier parts of his study. Two features stand out: Hayek is willing for government to provide a broad range of social services, in line with principles enunciated above; and he steadfastly opposes policies that aim at wealth redistribution or 'social justice'.

- In approaching *The Constitution of Liberty*, the reader must above all be prepared for surprises, regardless of his previous readings of the text. There are plenty of loose ends and undeveloped lines of reasoning in *The Constitution of Liberty*. A crucial concept that Hayek depends on but leaves undeveloped is that of 'the community'. Very much along Lockean lines, Hayek holds that the majority of a community, for its own protection, can authorise government to suspend civil liberties in emergency situations. But that is not all. The majority can authorise government to coerce citizens even when they have not violated the law. Leading examples are the military draft and the imposition of taxes. The implication here is that the community's interest is the highest end that government must seek, overriding the strict Rule of Law or in furtherance of it. Expedient policies are measured finally by the interest of the community. Another challenge in reading Hayek's text is to penetrate his theory of knowledge – one that views man's mind as 'a product of the civilization in which it has grown up'. Can Hayek avoid a thoroughgoing relativism and make room for universal or transcendent standards?

EDITORIAL NOTE

Some brief editorial points should be noted regarding this monograph. First, UK spelling conventions have been used in the general text. The quotations from *The Constitution of Liberty*, however, are taken from the original US version. As such, American-English conventions are used in these quotations. Second, where *The Constitution of Liberty* is referred to, the relevant page numbers are put in brackets after the reference. Where other works of F. A. Hayek are referred to, the author simply refers to the date of the work, followed by page numbers if appropriate. The relevant works by F. A. Hayek are then listed at the back of the monograph.

AUTHOR'S PREFACE

I take great pleasure in joining with the IEA to celebrate the fiftieth anniversary of the publication of F. A. Hayek's *The Constitution of Liberty*. Hayek had published important books and essay collections prior to this work and others would follow it; but *The Constitution of Liberty* continues to stand as the leading effort by any author, over the past century, to restate the principles of classical liberalism. Typically people read selected chapters from this grand work, especially its controversial Postscript; and the usual scholarly practice is to draw from it selectively to see how Hayek treats a particular problem over several of his writings or to trace the development of his thought. In fact, *The Constitution of Liberty* advances a careful argument that runs through the book from beginning to end: selective reading is likely to miss it.

Hayek's core argument is essentially about freedom and its value to the individual, to society and to civilisation at large. His approach requires him to define a condition of freedom and, in particular, to say what freedom is not. In order to show that freedom is something valuable, Hayek must consider both its intrinsic worth and its consequences, whether foreseen or unforeseen. Also, he must explain how a free society is different from an unfree one and, more broadly, how freedom contributes to human progress. In line with his desire to treat the question of freedom comprehensively, Hayek investigates the philosophical foundations of freedom and seeks to show how freedom can be established and preserved through the Rule of Law. Finally, he assesses a wide range of governmental policies in terms of their compatibility with freedom and their expediency.

Hayek's argument unfolds gradually; and the reader is sometimes caught by surprise when important new lines of thought are introduced without much notice. Also, there are unresolved tensions and loose ends in Hayek's argument that present interpretive difficulties. Hayek sometimes explores ideas that are not yet fully formed in his own mind, but which he will seek to clarify in later writings. For example, he will later present much more clearly the distinction among kinds of social order; the nature of rules; the meaning of justice; the character of evolution; and the shape of democratic governance. Undoubtedly there are important differences between *The Constitution of Liberty* and Hayek's later writings, but one should not assume that these are differences of principle. The later writings may simply clarify, expand or refine the argument of *The Constitution of Liberty* without abandoning its core principles. To decide this issue, one must obviously begin from *The Constitution of Liberty* itself and understand its basic argument.

Insofar as I know, no writer has yet followed carefully the central argument of *The Constitution of Liberty* and shown how it is developed in the various chapters of the book. My aim is to give a fresh account of this argument – one that will be fully accessible to the general reader and also useful to the Hayek scholar.

My original intention was to proceed chapter by chapter, but this proved to be impracticable. Some consolidation was required not only to hold my manuscript to a manageable length, but also to bring out the structure of Hayek's argument. In his opening chapters, Hayek interweaves observations about freedom with observations about knowledge. I treat freedom and knowledge thematically, in different sections, but with a view to their connection. Hayek takes up the problem of inequality at several points in his book, but I consolidate much of this in discussing Chapter 6. I consolidate several chapters in Part II on the origin and growth of the Rule of Law; and in covering what Hayek says in Part III on issues of policy, I look for common themes. To see how the order of my exposition compares with Hayek's, the reader will find it helpful to refer to Hayek's own table of contents, which can be found at the end of the book.[1]

The interpretive literature on Hayek is voluminous, and much of it is quite valuable; but if I should attempt to address it, a quite different book from the one intended would surely emerge. Thus I stick closely to the text of *The Constitution of Liberty* and to some related works by Hayek. Modern search engines, along with printed bibliographies, make it fairly easy to identify and often access the pertinent secondary literature on Hayek. For convenience I follow Hayek's practice of referring to humanity as 'man' and to the individual as 'he,' rather than switching to gender-neutral terminology.

I owe a debt of gratitude to many persons as well as to several institutions. I am grateful first of all to Hayek, who was one of my teachers in the University of Chicago's Committee on Social Thought. He also chaired my dissertation committee, whose other members were Leo Strauss and Joseph Cropsey. I first met Hayek at about the time that he was preparing *The Constitution of Liberty* for publication. Through the years I have received vital

---

1   This is not available in the online version.

instruction, wise guidance and welcome support from many friends. Chief among these are my colleagues in political science at the University of Georgia as well as the countless associates whom I have met and worked with through the activities of Liberty Fund, including the staff of that estimable foundation. There are special friends who, over the past year, provided generous encouragement as well as helpful advice as I worked on this manuscript. Above all I am grateful to my wife, Eva Miller, a cherished companion, who for more than five decades and sometimes at considerable sacrifice has made it possible for me to engage in a scholarly life.

Hayek's *The Constitution of Liberty*

1 HAYEK'S INTRODUCTION

The Constitution of Liberty begins with a 'Preface' and 'Introduction,' but the first thing to strike one's eye is the title itself. One might infer from it that Hayek intends to depict an institutional arrangement or framework of government that promotes liberty; but in fact the book says little about government's internal structure and operations. Later Hayek would clarify the meaning of his title: 'I then used the term "constitution" in the wide sense in which we use it also to describe the state of fitness of a person' (1973: 3). Hayek is concerned with liberty's present shape or condition – whether it is fit or unhealthy. Believing that liberty is in dire straits, he will diagnose the causes of its ill constitution and prescribe a remedy that might restore its fitness.

Hayek identifies liberty closely with Western civilisation. The principles of liberty or freedom – he uses these terms interchangeably (see 421) – grew out of the Western experience, and the West flourished by adhering to them. By the mid-nineteenth century, however, the West began to lose faith in the principles of liberty; and now it lacks firm beliefs on which to oppose threatening ideologies. In various writings Hayek emphasises one or another proximate danger to Western liberty – central planning, demands for social justice, excesses of majority rule – but the ultimate danger is this loss of faith and self-confidence. Hayek is especially harsh in his indictment of Western intellectuals, who have long been disillusioned with their own civilisation, disparaging of its achievements and drawn to utopianism. They turned away from Western principles just as other people of the world were looking to the West for guidance, leading the others to draw the wrong conclusions about liberty (1–2).

If the West is to continue on a path of progress, it must renew its understanding of liberty and liberty's value both to society and to individuals. To this end Hayek will identify the basic principles of liberty and restate them in words suited for today's climate of opinion. Hayek recognises that the task he has in mind must go beyond economics and historical inquiry. The contemporary situation requires attention to principles that claim 'universal validity.' It calls for an 'ultimate justification' or vindication of fundamental values. Economics and historical inquiry can certainly illuminate questions of liberty, but no single discipline has the comprehensiveness and normative force required to put liberty on a sound footing. This task is properly the work of 'political philosophy.' *The Constitution of Liberty* will undertake 'a comprehensive restatement of the basic principles of a philosophy of freedom' (3).

Hayek's discussion of freedom or liberty is divided into three main parts: The Value of Freedom; Freedom and the Law; and Freedom in the Welfare State. He explains that Part I 'endeavors to show why we want liberty and what it does.' Part II examines 'the institutions that Western man has developed to secure individual liberty.' Part III tests this ideal of liberty by applying its principles 'to some of today's critical economic and social issues' (5).

Hayek introduces several concepts in his Introduction that turn out to be much more important, as his argument unfolds, than might appear to be the case at first. I will say a bit about three of these: 'civilisation,' 'political philosophy,' and 'the ideal.'

Civilisation

Hayek sometimes refers to civilisations, in the plural, and he often speaks of the accomplishments of Western civilisation and the dangers it currently faces. More broadly, however, he understands civilisation as the most recent phase of man's social evolution. It began when men left 'primitive society' to adopt an urban way of life (340–41). The ceaseless and unguided process of social evolution, of which civilisation is a part, seems to be the basic reality for Hayek. Some thinkers in the liberal tradition, to say nothing of liberalism's German critics in the nineteenth and twentieth centuries, have distinguished sharply between ancient and modern civilisation, identifying modernity with the rise and flourishing of liberalism. Hayek rejects this bifurcation, since he wants to trace liberalism's core principles – individual freedom and the Rule of Law – to ancient traditions. Also, he appeals to older traditions in order to combat the most destructive features of modernity, which are associated in some measure with the rise of liberalism in the seventeenth century.

Hayek's approach raises several questions. Can the oft-discussed conflict between ancients and moderns be smoothed over in this way? Does Hayek's concept of a free and open society and its way of life retain what is vital to ancient thought – its elevation of noble virtues over useful ones? Does Hayek, in the final analysis, come down strongly on the side of modernity? Finally, how does Hayek relate what is particular in civilisations to what is universal? Can he praise the accomplishments of Western civilisation and tie civilisation's long-term prospects to its fate without adopting a parochial mentality?

Political philosophy

By the 1930s, Hayek's broad interests were taking him beyond technical questions in economics, but in a direction that his discoveries in economics were pointing to. Hayek's early work on the use of dispersed knowledge and the emergence of undesigned order (see Hayek, 1937) begins a transformation in Hayek's scholarly interests that reaches fruition in *The Constitution of Liberty*, where basic questions of political philosophy, especially moral questions, are forthrightly addressed. In the early 1940s, Hayek had understood his work as social science in the fashion of Max Weber (cf. Hayek, 1952b [1979]: 61–9; cf. 41–4). He had mentioned political philosophy from time to time, and by 1945 was moving in that direction (see Hayek, 1948: 2). Hayek's post-war writings, addresses and organisational efforts reflect a growing anxiety over the viability of Western civilisation and the fate of liberty, foreshadowing his deeper commitment to philosophical inquiry (see Hayek, 1992).

Political philosophy, as Hayek describes it in *The Constitution of Liberty*, has a practical as well as a theoretical side. A theoretical determination of basic principles is not enough. The philosopher must explain those principles to the general public, recommend them, make them attractive by showing their loveliness as well as their utility, and fight courageously against their enemies. Hayek justifies this practical undertaking by reference to the way opinion is formed in a free society and the way society progresses. Prevailing opinion is not the result of a deliberate decision by a majority or by an intellectual elite; instead, it grows out of a spontaneous and continuous process that elevates a minority view to a dominant position and then supplants it through the rise of another minority view (109–10). Discussion is essential finally to the emergence of the dominant view, but first people must learn about the alternatives by seeing individuals act them out.

But how do new ideas originate? The practical politician is necessarily 'unoriginal' in his beliefs. His task is to find the opinions held by the majority, and he moves within this framework. New ideas come from those few who professionally handle abstract ideas, and eventually their ideas shape majority opinion. Here Hayek quotes approvingly some well-known passages from J. S. Mill and J. M. Keynes to the effect that 'speculative philosophy' (Mill) or 'the ideas of economists and political philosophers' (Keynes) are, in the long run, far more powerful than interests in shaping thought and action. When judged only by his direct influence on current affairs, 'the influence of the political philosopher may be negligible,' but 'when his ideas have become common property, through the work of historians and publicists, teachers and writers, and intellectuals generally, they effectively guide developments' (112–13).

Hayek greatly elevates the philosopher's historical role by insisting that evolution is governed, in the long run, by 'ideas and therefore the men who give currency to new ideas.' He assigns importance not only to the innovators, but also to those thinkers who, along the way, provide 'a set of coherent conceptions' to govern the evolutionary process. Hayek's own objectives have to be understood in this light. He does not claim to be a great innovator, but rather one who restates old truths coherently. The political philosopher must address the question of what ought to be, deciding among conflicting values and defending those which seem right to him. The political philosopher should not seek popularity, but readily oppose the majority will when necessary by expressing 'inconvenient and irksome' truths. Indeed, he should 'suspect himself of failing in his task ... when he finds that his opinions are very popular' (115; cf. vii, 114–15). These characteristics – eyes focused on the long term, avidly defending sound values, unwilling to court popularity, insisting on unfashionable truths, persevering in the face of rejection, holding to the belief that the right ideas will eventually prevail – apply not only to the political philosopher, as Hayek describes him, but also to Hayek himself.

The ideal

Hayek refers time and again to the ideal. Recovering basic principles will help him to 'picture an ideal.' Hayek's emphasis on the ideal serves two purposes: it shows that liberty is something of high value; and it allows him to appeal to something above existing or possible arrangements that offers a criterion by which to judge them. As we shall see, Hayek's 'ideal' is the Rule of Law.

Generally Hayek's writings bring out the quixotic or dangerous side of idealism. In this very Introduction he reproaches Western intellectuals for their 'exclusive concern with the creation of "better worlds."' To forestall an immoderate pursuit of liberty, Hayek ends his Introduction by warning strongly against 'perfectionism.' Liberalism, properly understood, is far removed from 'the hurry and impatience of the passionate reformer.' It is 'a modest and even humble creed' with 'a low opinion of men's wisdom and capacities,' aware that even the best society we can plan for 'will not satisfy all our desires' (vii, 1–2, 6, 8).

Hayek's understanding of 'the ideal' raises a host of questions. How do ideals originate? Do we discover them or construct them? Are they grounded in what is real? In what sense, if at all, are ideals to be understood as transcendent? Can an ideal that is distilled from one culture or civilisation be binding for all? These questions will be explored in the course of our inquiry.

PART I
THE VALUE OF FREEDOM

2 INDIVIDUAL FREEDOM, COERCION AND PROGRESS (CHAPTERS 1–5 AND 9)

Hayek starts by defining a state of liberty or freedom: 'We are concerned in this book with that condition of men in which coercion of some by others is reduced as much as is possible in society' (11). Who are the 'some' who must be protected from coercion, and who are the 'others' who must be restrained? By what means can coercion in society be reduced, and how much of it will necessarily remain? These are questions that Hayek wrestles with throughout *The Constitution of Liberty*.

Individual freedom and responsibility

Freedom, for Hayek, belongs to individual human beings. There are several reasons why he begins from 'the individual.'

First, the human individual is the being that chooses, thinks and acts; and it is primarily to such an agent that the concept of freedom properly applies. Hayek acknowledges that human agency raises perplexing questions about the individual's capacity to choose or to will freely; but in defining a condition of freedom, it suffices to consider only external impediments to action as they might arise not from nature, but from other human beings.

Second, freedom must be defined by reference to individuals. Hayek believes that he is recovering the earliest understanding of freedom when he defines it as '[t]he state in which a man is not subject to coercion by the arbitrary will of another or others' (11). This definition goes back to the earliest distinction between slaves and free men; and it has been affirmed by the best modern proponents of liberty, who insist on a free private sphere, defined by clear rules and protected from arbitrary coercion, in which the individual may pursue his own aims, so long as his actions do not violate the freedom of others. Hayek concedes that he is advancing a 'negative' view of freedom (the absence of coercion), but he also insists that such freedom takes on a 'positive' character through the use that individuals make of it (19).

Third, a free society cannot exist without free individuals and, as Hayek will go on to argue, this requires freedom for all. Some collectivist teachings have posited a social or political freedom that excludes individual freedom, but Hayek strongly rejects any effort to divorce the two.

Hayek acknowledges that freedom has acquired meanings that are quite different from the one he prefers. Individual freedom should not be confused with 'political freedom,' understood as a people's consenting to a government, participating in legislation, or controlling administration. Popular consent and participation won't necessarily secure individual freedom and may work against it (13–15).

Again, individual freedom is not to be understood as exercising free will or choosing one's course of action and sticking to it. In defining a condition of freedom, the question is whether others can impose their will on me, not whether I can follow my own will. Hayek recognises, however, that the problem of free will is an important one; and he returns to it in Chapter 5, where he discusses responsibility.

Hayek insists that liberty and responsibility cannot be

separated. Liberty requires that the individual 'must bear the consequences of his actions' (71). Without responsibility in this sense, individuals would be unable to learn from their experiences and to enjoy personal growth. Moreover, a free society 'will not function or maintain itself unless its members regard it as right that each individual occupy the position that results from his action and accept it as due to his own action' (71). Scientific determinism teaches, however, that actions result not from one's own free choice, but from circumstances beyond one's control; and many believe that this scientific teaching has destroyed the basis for individual responsibility.

Hayek does not reject determinism altogether. The conception of responsibility 'rests, in fact, on a determinist view' – the view that actions follow from such 'internal' causes as emotion and habit (73). This raises the question of 'inner freedom,' or whether internal causes deprive actions of their voluntary character. Hayek does not pursue this question, since he is concerned with a determinist teaching that looks to external rather than internal causes of action. This form of determinism is an offshoot of nineteenth-century physics. It holds that our actions and mental operations are necessarily determined by material circumstances 'external' to the actor.

In refuting scientific determinism, Hayek does not try to show that it is false, but only that it is wrong pragmatically. It conflicts with what we believe to be the case when we urge people to observe certain rules. Experience leads me to believe that my admonitions will make a difference in a person's conduct, and I want that person to believe that he should choose the responsible path; but the truth is that neither of us knows whether free choice is possible or whether praise and blame can make a difference (72–6).

Finally, individual freedom is not to be identified with the power to overcome obstacles or to satisfy one's wishes. The idea of 'liberty as power' translates easily into a demand for power or wealth, as opposed to freedom from coercion (see 13–18).

The individual and society

Hayek's opening approach may suggest that he holds a radically individualistic view of man, but this judgement would be premature and mistaken. As we shall discover, Hayek goes very far in emphasising our dependence on society and the need to understand individual actions in light of social relationships. We experience other persons in their concreteness and individuality, but never apart from their qualities as social beings.

Hayek's 'individual' is thus a deliberate abstraction from social man and the social context of human life. Hayek begins this way in order to establish that freedom is the individual's enjoyment of an assured private sphere, safe from interference by others and especially from arbitrary coercion by government. It will turn out that the human being's involvement in society and his membership in a particular community also raise vital issues of coercion; but in defining freedom, Hayek wants to defer consideration of these issues, and he achieves this by abstracting from man's social and communal relations.

Hayek's insistence on the social character of human life shapes his understanding of the liberal tradition and his own place in it. Hayek emphatically rejects the 'rationalist' understanding of the individual and society, which many have identified as the original and primary form of liberalism. Rationalist theory, as characterised by Hayek, is some blend of John Locke's ideas, especially as interpreted by Locke's followers in England, France and America, and aspects of Bentham's utilitarianism. The rationalists start from the idea of natural liberty, insisting that freedom is each individual's birthright. Moreover, man enjoyed the gift of reason from the beginning. Man was 'originally endowed with both the intellectual and the moral attributes that enabled him to fashion civilization deliberately' (59). Morals, language and law were inventions of 'an independently and antecedently existing human reason' (57). Living freely in the 'state of nature' and employing their reason, men proceeded to design their civil institutions, perhaps by entrusting the task to a wise legislator or by entering into a social contract. All useful institutions, including the state, are 'deliberate contrivances.' The rationalists 'cannot conceive of anything serving a human purpose that has not been consciously designed' (61).

In Hayek's estimation, these teachings are both erroneous and dangerous. They fail to recognise the limits of reason and the social dimensions of liberty. To frame his own account of liberal principles, Hayek draws on an 'anti-rationalist' or 'empiricist evolutionary tradition' that grew out of English common law, Scottish moral philosophy and the reflections of parliamentarians such as Edmund Burke. This exposition gives Hayek an opportunity to bring out the social side of human life.

The anti-rationalists rejected the idea that man is born free, or that freedom is man's original or natural condition. Human beings lived from the beginning in societies that were built around the family. Civilisation was not the product of rational design, but 'the accumulated hard-earned result of trial and error' (60). Freedom could develop only after civilisation had tamed and checked 'man's more primitive and ferocious instincts' (60).

Moreover, civilisation was necessary to man's development as a rational being, for 'human reason has grown and can successfully operate' only with and within the framework of morals, language and law. It follows that free institutions were not constructed to fit some rational conception of freedom. Free institutions evolved first, and conceptions of liberty came later as these institutions were studied (57–60).

When Hayek refers to 'classical liberalism,' he means the form it took in the nineteenth century, after the anti-rationalism of thinkers such as Hume, Adam Smith and Burke became widely influential. His broad aim is to recover and restate classical liberalism as thus understood. Besides emphasising the social dimension of human life, classical liberalism developed ideas about markets that Adam Smith and other evolutionists had put forward. It did not envision unbridled individualism or complete laissez-faire – a doctrine that belongs to the French rationalist tradition and was never defended by any of the English classical economists. The evolutionists' argument was 'never antistate as such, or anarchistic.' It 'accounted both for the proper functions of the state and for the limits of state action' (60; cf. 1973: 61–2; 1976: 54).

Limiting state coercion

Hayek acknowledges that his definition of freedom is incomplete so long as coercion remains undefined. He thus examines various ways of defining coercion, but the deeper question is why it is desirable for the individual to have a sphere of freedom in which coercion is reduced to a minimum.

Unlike romantics who imagine that society can flourish

without coercive government, Hayek insists that state coercion is required to prevent private persons from coercing each other (21). This does not mean that all private coercion can be eliminated. Hayek grants, for example, that coercion of a subtle kind – psychological pressures to give in to another's moods or demands – often occurs in private relationships that individuals enter into voluntarily, but for the state to regulate or restrict such choices would involve even greater coercion: 'if people are to be free to choose their associates and intimates, the coercion that arises from voluntary association cannot be the concern of government' (138).

The state monopolises coercion under all forms of government; but in a free society, the exercise of government's coercive power is constrained and made predictable by general rules that apply equally to all individuals, including those who make and enforce the laws. Conformity to law is the primary safeguard against arbitrary government – a point that Hayek will develop at length in discussing the Rule of Law. We note that while the law is constraining, it is not in itself coercive.

Coercion by the state is indispensable to freedom, but Hayek wants to reduce the need for it to a minimum. This is possible only where individuals can be expected to conform voluntarily to traditional rules of conduct and, in particular, to common moral rules. Evolved moral rules, as distinct from synthetically constructed ones, should thus be regarded with reverence and held as a matter of sincere belief. Hayek follows 'all the great apostles of freedom outside the rationalistic school' in emphasising that 'freedom has never worked without deeply ingrained moral beliefs' (62).

Is our conformity to moral rules truly voluntary, or is it simply produced by a different kind of coercion or compulsion to that imposed by the state? As Hayek explains it, we conform to moral rules mostly from habit, but social pressure to do so is often intense. J. S. Mill had regarded such conformity as the most pressing contemporary threat to freedom, greater even than the threat of state coercion (Mill, 1975: 57–69). Hayek is less concerned than Mill with protecting private conduct 'from the pressure of opinion or disapproval.' Mill, in strongly attacking this so-called moral coercion, 'probably overstated the case for liberty' (146; cf. 435, n. 32). In Hayek's view, it is better 'not to represent as coercion the pressure that public approval or disapproval exerts to secure obedience to moral rules and conventions' (146).

Hayek thinks that 'a free society will function successfully only if the individuals are in some measure guided by common values;' and this is why he is willing for society to exert pressure on individuals to conform to moral rules. Nonetheless, he doesn't want this pressure to interfere with the individual's freedom of choice. We must recognise that 'each person has his own scale of values which we ought to respect, even if we do not approve of it.' If we believe in freedom, we will not 'regard ourselves as the ultimate judges of another person's values' or 'feel entitled to prevent him from pursuing ends which we disapprove of so long as he does not infringe the equally protected sphere of others.' A society that fails to recognise these principles 'can have no respect for the dignity of the individual and cannot really know freedom' (79).

Freedom of action

What is to count as coercion, especially the arbitrary kind that encroaches on individual freedom? Hayek certainly wishes to protect individuals and their property from physical harm, but his primary emphasis is on assuring the individual's freedom of action. Inflicting physical harm, or threatening it, is a form of coercion, but so is interference with free action. Freedom of action includes economic liberty, but it is wider than this. For Hayek, it encompasses the individual's freedom to plan his own life and to carry out that plan. Recognising that this requires extensive information, Hayek defines coercion broadly to include the manipulation of a person's environment by such means as deception or withholding vital facts. Coercion, in this wider sense, is 'the control of the essential data of an individual's action by another' (139).

In extending this freedom to every individual, Hayek implicitly follows the principle, famously articulated by Kant, that human individuals are to be regarded as ends and not as a means only. A person who is coerced no longer pursues his own ends or plan of life, but must act according to ends or goals that are imposed by someone else. In so acting I become merely a means to another's end. I still exercise choice, but 'my mind is made someone else's tool, because the alternatives before me have been so manipulated that the conduct that the coercer wants me to choose becomes for me the least painful one' (133). I have been deprived of the use of my intelligence and knowledge in the pursuit of my own aims (134).

But why is it beneficial that the individual should be free to pursue his own ends or life plan? Hayek is somewhat vague about the benefit that the individual himself gains from such freedom. He does not justify it as a path to success in amassing property, winning acclaim, cultivating virtue, or attaining happiness: 'we must recognize that we may be free and yet miserable' (18). Hayek requires a justification that upholds freedom even if the individual is unsuccessful in attaining his ends or, should he succeed, finds their attainment unappealing. His solution is to emphasise the value of striving and learning:

> What matters is the successful striving for what at each
> moment seems attainable. It is not the fruits of past
> success but the living in and for the future in which
> human intelligence proves itself. Progress is movement for
> movement's sake, for it is in the process of learning, and
> in the effects of having learned something new, that man
> enjoys the gift of his intelligence. (41)

This principle – that progress is continuous striving and learning – applies both to the individual and to humanity at large.

Freedom and progress

Individuals cherish freedom of action and benefit personally from it, but Hayek's case for individual freedom rests on broader considerations: 'It is not because we like to be able to do particular things, not because we regard any particular freedom as essential to our happiness, that we have a claim to freedom' (32). Hayek's broader argument for individual freedom comes to light particularly in Chapters 2 and 3, where he emphasises its contribution to society at large and to the progress of civilisation.

Hayek prepares the ground for this broader argument by insisting that I may benefit much more from the way other individuals use their freedom than from how I use my own. In fact, the benefits which I derive from freedom are 'largely the result of the uses of freedom by others, and mostly of those uses of freedom that I could never avail myself of' (32). The useful contributions of even a few individuals can be of immense value to their contemporaries. Indeed, the freedom 'that will be used by only one man in a million may be more important to society and more beneficial to the majority than any freedom that we all use' (31). This result does not require disinterested or benevolent actions, although it may proceed from such motives. Typically the actor, in seeking to benefit himself, also benefits unknown persons without intending to do so or foreseeing this result.

Hayek continues this argument by calling attention, as he often does, to our fundamental ignorance. I can never know which particular individuals will use their freedom so as to benefit me and the rest of society. Certainly I cannot identify in advance that 'one man in a million' whose contribution will be immense. Hayek describes freedom as 'opportunity for the unknown few' (533). Only by extending freedom as broadly as possible can we provide an opportunity for these unknown benefactors to use their freedom effectively. Since no one has sufficient knowledge to pick and choose such individuals, freedom must be given to all.

From here Hayek proceeds to show that individual freedom is essential to the long-term growth of civilisation and the advance of humanity at large. The progress of civilisation depends on man's freedom to experiment with new ways of doing things. Here again, no one can predict in advance which 'experiment in living' will move civilisation ahead. Progress cannot be designed: 'it is not achieved by human reason striving by known means toward a fixed aim.' Progress 'always leads into the unknown.' At most we can only expect 'to gain an understanding of the kind of forces' that bring about undesigned growth and try to create conditions that are favourable to it (40).

Earlier we took note of Hayek's insistence that a free society is a traditional society – one whose members regard their evolved traditions with respect and even reverence. Yet if a society is to survive and grow, it must adapt to changing conditions; and this requires freedom to experiment and innovate. Some individuals or groups must deviate from or go beyond established rules and try something new. Civilisation grows through a process of trial and error, and innovators are indispensable to this process.

Innovation begins as a response to changes in a society's material environment. Some of these changes can be dealt with by temporarily adjusting practices and resource use, while others will require lasting modifications in tools and institutions (32–3). When Hayek speaks of adaptation (a central concept in his account of social evolution), he has these latter cases primarily in mind. Without innovation, our adaptation to changing circumstances would be impossible. Innovation introduces new ways of doing things. These new ways compete with old ones and with each other. If a new way proves to be effective, others may imitate it. As Hayek explains, 'the selection by imitation of successful institutions and habits' is decisive for social evolution (59). Society's growth in the past has depended on an unconscious process of trying new things, learning, imitation, selection and adaptation; and this remains largely true even with the emergence of reason.

Hayek explains intellectual progress in terms of this broader process of social evolution. Advances in thought depend fundamentally on man's unconscious adaptation to changed material conditions and thus on freedom of action. Intellectual liberty – freedom of thought, research and communication – is 'significant only in the last stage of the process in which new truths are discovered.' Scientists understand that intellectual progress results from new ideas; and most realise that advances in knowledge cannot be planned in advance, since they 'often spring from the unforeseen and undesigned.' What they are apt to overlook is that new ideas depend on innovative actions and thus on 'the freedom of *doing* things.' In Hayek's view, the intellectual process 'is in effect only a process of elaboration, selection, and elimination of ideas already formed' in our daily conduct of practical affairs. The flow of new ideas 'to a great extent, springs from the sphere in which action, often non-rational action, and material events impinge upon each other.' It would 'dry up if freedom were confined to the intellectual sphere.' Since thinking depends on doing, '[f]reedom of action, even in humble things, is as important as freedom of thought' (33–5).

Progress as radical change

The Constitution of Liberty might leave the impression that progress is mostly gradual, smooth and cumulative. Does Hayek recognise that progress often involves sharp discontinuities, destructive negations and radical transformations?

Hegel's dialectical account of history offers one such view of progress. Hayek emphatically rejects the Hegelian dialectic, especially as it is restated by Marx, but without specifically criticising the idea that progress occurs through negation and sublation. His attack centres instead on Hegel's rationalism and determinism, i.e. the insistence that historical progress is governed by a fixed law that is both necessary in its operations and intelligible to reason. The main features of Hayek's own evolutionary theory – no determining law, the indispensability of free action, no known goal of progress, the impossibility of understanding fully how progress works or making specific predictions about its direction

– are intended to counter Hegelian and Marxist dialectics (Hayek, 1952b [1979]: 367–400).

Another challenge to the idea that progress flows smoothly – one that avoids Hegelian assumptions about a fixed law of progress – can be found in some influential depictions of modern technology. These hold that social change is driven by the relentless advance of innovative technologies that inevitably undermine obsolete customs and institutions. Joseph Schumpeter, who developed an early version of this view, famously spoke of technological advance as 'creative destruction,' thereby incorporating both Marx's theory of revolution and Nietzsche's insistence that the creative individual – the innovator – must also be a destroyer (see Schumpeter, 1950: 31–2, 41–3, 81–6; Nietzsche, 1954: 170–72). Modern technology, thus understood, would seem to be at odds with traditional society of the kind Hayek favours.

Hayek grants that modern progress depends on the rapid advance of technology, which inevitably leaves destruction in its wake, thus producing losers as well as winners. He had noted this earlier in describing the Industrial Revolution and the social alterations it produced in England. While benefiting the great majority of workers, the Industrial Revolution 'destroyed' the privileged position and power of the upper classes and endangered 'certain aesthetic and moral values' to which these classes attached great importance (1954: 25–7). Hayek grants that most people are likely to be averse to progress, since while 'bringing them much they strive for,' progress also 'forces on them many changes they do not want at all.' The point, however, is that the spread of technology has 'largely deprived us of the choice as to whether or not we want continued rapid progress' (51–2).

Why are Westerners today 'not only the creatures but the

captives of progress'? Why does 'the peace of the world and, with it civilization itself ... depend on continued progress at a fast rate'? Hayek concludes Chapter 4 by warning that advanced technology, vital to the West's prosperity, can be turned against it in the form of destructive weaponry. Hayek is not proposing an arms race, but rather making a demonstration of technology's promise. A great proportion of the world's people, dissatisfied with their own lot, think they can prosper by redistributing Western wealth – a belief that reflects the influence of Western ideas. Moreover, the spread of technology has given these disgruntled peoples a new power to destroy Western nations; and '[a]s their strength grows, they will become able to extort such redistribution' unless the West can show that the best way to increase overall wealth is through peaceful progress (52–3).

3 THE USE AND LIMITS OF KNOWLEDGE (CHAPTERS 2, 3, 4)

Hayek's teaching on human knowledge provides the foundation for his political philosophy. His key concepts are defined substantially by reference to knowing. Liberty is having access to the information needed to design and follow one's plan of life. Tradition is knowledge in the form of accumulated experience. Progress is the advance of knowledge. For Hayek, determining what we cannot know – the limits to human knowledge – is as important as discovering what is knowable. Time and again he calls attention to our fundamental ignorance and builds arguments around our lack of knowledge. In fact, he insists that the 'case for individual freedom rests chiefly on the recognition of the inevitable ignorance of all of us concerning a great many of the factors on which the achievement of our ends and welfare depends' (29).

Reflections on knowledge appear throughout Chapters 2, 3 and 4 of *The Constitution of Liberty*, interwoven with themes that we considered in the previous chapter. The task now is to reconstruct Hayek's teaching on knowledge and explore its key elements. Hayek had long argued that the individual possesses only a small amount of the knowledge required for success in daily life and thus must 'make use of more knowledge than he has himself acquired' (22). In the first two sections of this chapter, I consider the mechanisms that make available for our use the knowledge possessed by others. Our using others' knowledge is possible because individuals participate in an order that they did not create and whose ultimate workings they cannot understand. Thus in the third section I examine Hayek's discussion of order – how it originates and works to our advantage. The fourth section explores Hayek's account of reason and shows how it rests on his evolutionary conception of mind. The concluding sections consider how knowledge is embodied in traditions, values and moral rules.

Using inherited knowledge: rules and traditions

What specific mechanisms make it possible for us to use the knowledge of others? Hayek makes a start on identifying these mechanisms near the beginning of Chapter 2, where he distinguishes between 1) 'the transmission in time of our accumulated stock of knowledge,' and 2) 'the communication among contemporaries of information on which they base their action' (27). The difference, viewed from the actor's standpoint, is this: past knowledge becomes available for use largely by our conforming to rules, while we make use of contemporaneous knowledge largely by responding to signs.

In the West particularly, the advance of science is a conspicuous and vital way in which knowledge is transmitted through time; but from the standpoint of man's evolution, the transmission of various tools, customs and institutions has been much more important. All these examples involve a compliance with rules. Hayek insists that rule-governed behaviour long preceded the use of reason and language, so it need not be deliberate or even something of which one is conscious. For a very long time rules were no more than behavioural dispositions. Their articulation in speech and in writing came very late in the process of human evolution; and even now, our compliance with rules has mostly a subconscious and habitual character.

Hayek frames the story of human evolution in terms of the genesis, diffusion and transmission of rules. Elements of this story appear in *The Constitution of Liberty*, but it is presented much more clearly in later writings. In his most detailed account of the matter, Hayek identifies three stages of evolution, each of which involves rule-governed behaviour, but with great variation in both the character of the rules and the behaviour itself. This account is necessarily conjectural, since it looks back at least a million years, long before the beginnings of recorded history.

Hayek speculates that primitive society consisted of small bands of 15 to 40 persons, who lived by hunting and gathering. Its rules were nothing more than instinctive dispositions to act in ways that favoured group solidarity and survival. How did general rules emerge? Hayek attaches great importance to the mind's facility of treating particulars as members of a class – what he calls 'abstraction.' Verbal statements are a clear example, but so are our behavioural responses. Abstraction 'manifests itself also in the way in which we respond similarly to any one of a class of events which in most respects may be very different from one another, and the feelings which are evoked by those events and which guide our action, be it a sense of justice or of moral or aesthetic approval or disapproval' (40, 452, n. 4; cf. Hayek, 1952a: 142–6; and Hayek, 1978a: 35–49). This subconscious, responsive form of abstraction developed as human beings moved through different social structures; and the most efficient of these abstract behavioural rules were spread through imitation (observers acquired the rule by imitating particular actions that exemplified it) and were enforced by social pressures. The verbal articulation of learnt rules began about eight thousand years ago, and written codes of morality and law are much more recent. Even after these developments, subconscious abstraction would continue to exert a dominant influence on human action (see 61–7, 148–9, 151–2; Hayek, 1973: 17–21, 74–6; Hayek, 1979: 159–61).

Our present stock of knowledge consists in large degree of rules that we have acquired through habit, custom and tradition. Social evolution tends to be cumulative, so that traces of earlier rules are brought forward into the present, where they exist in a layered or stratified form.

Using contemporaneous knowledge: imitation, prices and esteem

Transmission in time is one of the ways by which knowledge becomes available for our use. The other way is through communication among contemporaries, three examples of which are: a) 'individuals imitating those who have been more successful;' b) individuals being guided by 'prices offered for their products;' and c) individuals responding to 'expressions of moral or aesthetic esteem for their having observed standards of conduct' (28–9). All three processes are vital to civilisation. Imitation is essential to society's adaptive evolution, where 'the decisive factor is not the selection of the physical and inheritable properties of the individuals but the selection by imitation of successful institutions and habits' (59). Prices convey vital information about the economic behaviour of dispersed individuals. Signs of approval or disapproval promote conformity to rules.

Hayek had long been interested in the way prices convey information. In writings dating back to the 1930s, he had emphasised the indispensability of prices to economic life (see 1948: 33–56). The most influential of these writings is his 1945 essay 'The Use of Knowledge in Society.' This essay takes up 'the economic problem of society' and argues that it 'can be solved, and in fact is being solved, by the price system' (ibid.: 77, 85). Hayek points out that rapid adaptation to social change requires knowledge of the particular circumstances of time and place; but this knowledge, which is dispersed among countless individuals, cannot be concentrated in a single mind or planning board. The problem then is to find a way to put dispersed knowledge to use for everyone's advantage. In a free society, the price system solves this problem by ensuring 'that the knowledge of the particular circumstances of time and place will be promptly utilized.' Moreover, it communicates to the individual 'such further information as he needs to fit his decisions into the whole pattern of changes of the larger economic system' (83–4). Hayek concludes by observing that the economic problem is but part of a broader one, i.e. the need for processes to overcome 'the unavoidable imperfection of man's knowledge' (91). Indeed, this broader problem 'arises in connection with nearly all truly social phenomena, with language and most of our cultural inheritance, and constitutes really the central theoretical problem of all social science' (88).

Hayek here anticipates the more comprehensive treatment of the use of knowledge that he offers in *The Constitution of Liberty* (see 4). As it turns out, attentiveness to prices is one way, but not the only way, that we overcome the imperfection of our knowledge by making use of what others know. In fact, *The Constitution of Liberty* has much more to say about imitation and about the salience of moral approval and disapproval than about the price mechanism.

In the 1945 essay, and sometimes also in *The Constitution of Liberty*, Hayek employs this interesting formulation: the price system allows the individual to use knowledge that he does not possess; prices signal what countless individuals know of their own local situations; and I can use them in my own calculations without actually possessing the dispersed knowledge that they reflect. Whether this formulation would also cover our use of traditional rules as well as instances of communication other than the price system (imitation, responding to signs of approval and disapproval) is uncertain. In conforming to tradition, arguably we would possess the rule either as a subconscious habit or as a conscious precept, although the reasons for the rule – the experiences from which it originated and through which it survived a long process of cultural selection – are unknown to us and therefore not in our possession. For the most part rules are followed blindly, without consideration of the reasons for them. The same may be largely true of our responses to approval and disapproval. Hayek does indicate, however, that as social evolution advances, imitation may come to have an element of deliberation and choice.

Knowledge and social order

In daily life we rely on rules and signs and take for granted the knowledge they make available for our use. By acting on such knowledge, we are able to carry out our own plans and to anticipate what to expect from others. All of this is to assume that the social world is orderly, but where does this order come from and what is its character?

Accounting for order is a central aim of Hayek's political philosophy, but his discussion of it in *The Constitution of Liberty* is quite diffuse as compared with later presentations, where he distinguishes quite clearly between the order that men deliberately make ('organisation') and order that forms itself ('spontaneous order'). Both kinds of order are essential to civilisation (see 1964).

Hayek is widely known for his advocacy of the idea of spontaneous order. He briefly discusses the concept itself at two points in *The Constitution of Liberty*, although the idea of spontaneous growth is present in his discussions of tradition, liberty and progress. Hayek's comments about organisation as a source of order are scattered elsewhere in the book, so the relationship of spontaneous and constructed order is not developed thematically.

Hayek's first description of spontaneous order, though not by that name, comes in Chapter 4, where he examines the contribution of eighteenth-century British thinkers to our understanding of progress. These thinkers, especially David Hume, Adam Smith and Adam Ferguson, addressed the following question: how can social order emerge, if not from a designing human intelligence or that of a superior being? In addressing it, they

> showed how, in the relations among men, complex and orderly and, in a very definite sense, purposive institutions might grow up which owed little to design, which were not invented but arose from the separate actions of many men who did not know what they were doing. (58–9)

The Scots in particular saw that the orderly growth of institutions takes place through 'adaptive evolution' or 'the survival of the successful' (59, 57). Those tools and institutions survive which have proven themselves superior (60). This insight was central to the British case for freedom, which held that the value of freedom 'consists mainly in the opportunity it provides for the growth of the undesigned' (61).

It must be emphasised that in embracing the idea of evolution, Hayek has in mind social or cultural evolution as anticipated in the teachings of eighteenth-century thinkers, particularly the Scots, and not physical evolution as taught later by Charles Darwin and others. What is crucial to cultural evolution is not the selection and transmission of physical characteristics, but rather the selection and transmission of values or rules of conduct. Cultural evolution takes place through a process of 'winnowing and sifting,' and where it will lead is unknowable and thus unpredictable. Certainly it does not exhibit an intelligible law. Its tendency, however, is to produce orders or structures that reflect 'the differential advantages gained by groups from practices adopted for some unknown and perhaps purely accidental reasons' (1979: 155; cf. 153–9, 196–200).

Hayek returns to spontaneous order at the very end of Chapter 10, where he draws a parallel between natural and social order. Often in the physical world we must 'rely on the spontaneous adjustments of individual elements to produce a physical order.' For example, we 'could never produce a crystal or a complex organic compound if we had to place each individual molecule or atom in the appropriate place in relation to the others;' yet because the individual molecules or atoms obey a law of nature, they will in certain conditions 'arrange themselves in a structure possessing certain characteristics' (160). Hayek reasons that spontaneous forces can likewise produce human society when individuals act in accordance with general rules or laws. Lawmakers can promote social order by establishing the conditions for it, but cannot do so by trying to arrange individuals in an orderly way. Thus the lawmaker's task 'is not to set up a particular order but merely to create conditions in which an orderly arrangement can establish and ever renew itself' (161).

Hayek draws support here from Michael Polanyi, who speaks of 'the spontaneous formation of a "polycentric order."' Polanyi explains that such order 'is achieved among human beings by allowing them to interact with each other on their own initiative – subject only to the laws which uniformly apply to all of them.' Their individual efforts are coordinated 'by exercising their individual initiative;' and 'this self-coordination justifies this liberty on public grounds' (160).

As for deliberate organisation, Hayek acknowledges that a free society 'produces institutions in which, for those who prefer it, a man's advancement depends on the judgment of some superior or of the majority of his fellows.' Business firms and government agencies would be leading examples of such institutions. Here individuals are subject to the orders of their superiors, and their place in the organisation depends on someone else's judgement of their contribution or their merit (99).

Hayek emphasises that his argument for liberty 'is not an argument against organization, which is one of the most powerful means that human reason can employ.' What he principally objects to are, first, monopolistic organisations that are exclusive, privileged and coercive, and second, any attempt to impose on society at large the organisational pattern, with individuals being assigned to positions according to a single comprehensive scale of merit. He faults the French rationalist tradition in particular for seeking 'the highest degree of political civilization in *organization*, that is, in the highest degree of interference by public power' (55). So long as the growth of organisations 'does not produce a situation in which a single comprehensive scale of merit is imposed upon the whole society, so long as a multiplicity of organizations compete with one another in offering different prospects, this is not merely compatible with freedom but extends the range of choice open to the individual' (99).

The wide availability of useful knowledge, as transmitted through rules and communicated though signs, attests to an order that, while not intelligible itself, is the source of intelligibility in our daily lives. This order, speaking broadly, is what Hayek means by 'civilisation,' understood as the direction of man's social evolution since the advent of cities, about eight thousand years ago. Civilisation is an artificial order, generated spontaneously by countless individual actions but not designed or instituted by anyone. It requires adaptations to material conditions that nature imposes, but is not a product of natural growth. Organisations play an indispensable role within this undesigned order, but can never hope to replace it.

Reason, mind and civilisation

Hayek seeks to defend reason, properly understood, against rationalism: 'Reason undoubtedly is man's most precious possession,' but it has been abused by persons who greatly exaggerate its powers (69). In *The Constitution of Liberty*, Hayek uses the term 'anti-rationalist' to identify his preferred position (see 57, 61, 63, 69, 437), but as he came to recognise, this usage obscures his true intention. After all, Britain's so-called anti-rationalists were not opposed to reason, but wanted to make reason more effective by establishing its proper limits. Thus in later writings he drops this term, declaring it to be a dangerous and misleading expression that ought to be avoided. The rationalist/anti-rationalist distinction is replaced by one between two kinds of rationalism, which Hayek calls 'constructivist' and 'critical.' His own position, and that of the evolutionary tradition from which he draws, is renamed 'critical rationalism' – a term borrowed from Karl Popper (1967: 94).

In order to bring out reason's limits, Hayek offers a critique of reason. This critique moves at two levels, one of which is much more radical than the other. At the less radical level, Hayek insists on the pervasiveness of human ignorance and shows that reason can neither supply the knowledge required for daily life nor explain the processes that make such knowledge available for our use. At a second and more damaging level, he depreciates reason itself, first by subordinating reason to the subconscious mind and then by submerging mind into the process of civilisation.

Hayek knew that rationalism, both ancient and modern, had taken its bearings by a natural order whose principles are constant and intelligible to the human mind. In one way or another, it had taught that reason can transcend the here and now, the opinions of the time, to apprehend the unchanging truth of things, including the good and beautiful. Ancient and medieval rationalists in particular had taught that essential qualities of the world itself are captured by the concepts employed in reasoning. Knowledge of nature, especially human nature, would provide a timeless standard by reference to which human affairs could be ordered. Hayek regards these rationalist views as both wrong theoretically and dangerous from a practical standpoint. He wants to foreclose any appeal to nature that might call tradition into question, or undercut the existing order, or fuel reckless change by stimulating a taste for 'perfectionism.'

Hayek aims to discredit rationalist theories of this sort through his evolutionary account of mind. By his account, the human mind evolved slowly for a million years or more before reason finally emerged. Even now, our actions depend much more on habit and unthinking responses to signs than on the kind of knowledge that an individual mind 'consciously manipulates' (24). Man's mind is thus 'a product of the civilization in which he has grown up and ... he is unaware of much of the experience which has shaped it – experience that assists it by being embodied in the habits, conventions, language, and moral beliefs which are part of its makeup' (24). What mind has and will become depend on the process of civilisation. Civilisation preserves and transmits general rules and beliefs, and the individual mind is a collection of them. This is not to say that the mind is merely passive. Besides classifying sense data, it has 'the capacity to restrain instincts.' Without such restraints, civilisation could never develop (1988: 22; cf. 1979: 160).

Hayek was greatly influenced by the historicisation of the mind that occurred in German thought in the late nineteenth century – a development that would, over the next century, transform the way scholars understood human knowing and reasoning. This was a time when historians and anthropologists were able to argue, from abundant data, that beliefs and world-views vary greatly from one society or civilisation to another. Such data alone was insufficient, however, to support the claim that the mind itself changes. For this a theory of knowledge was required.

This new theory began from Kant's principle that ultimate being is unknowable to reason, because we perceive it only as filtered through the mind's categories. Nature, as known to us, is already a product of a mental transformation and not a true picture of ultimate being. Hayek himself presents such a view in *The Sensory Order*. The individual mind is here described as a complex of relations in the central nervous system that classifies sense perceptions according to some interpretive framework. This means that sense data are never perceived by us in a raw or direct form. What we perceive are things with distinct qualities; and such perceptions have already been formed by the mind's classificatory and interpretive operations. The mind's perceptions of reality are necessarily interpretations in line with some classificatory scheme (see 1952a; also Miller, 1972: 250–64).

Radical historicism, however, took a second and more far-reaching step. If the mind is essentially historical, this means that the categories of thought also change, so that reality itself is understood differently according to time and place. Moreover, there is no final or privileged epoch of the kind Hegel posits, in which reason reaches perfection by understanding the historical process as a whole. Human thought necessarily understands reality from some point of view. There are many such viewpoints, and no particular one has a justifiable claim to finality.

In his writings from the 1940s and early 1950s, Hayek strongly opposes the historicist claim that 'the human mind is itself variable' and holds instead that 'all mind must run in terms of certain universal categories of thought' (1952b [1979]: 133, 136). In *The Constitution of Liberty*, however, Hayek appears to change course, declaring that man's mind 'is itself a system that constantly changes as a result of his endeavor to adapt himself to his surroundings' (23). A few years later, he explains that 'man's capacity to think is not a natural endowment of the individual but a cultural heritage, something transmitted not biologically but through example and teaching – mainly through, and implicit in, the teaching of language.' Much more than we are yet aware of, language probably 'determines our whole manner of thinking and our view and interpretation of the world.' Our language furnishes us with a 'picture of the world' or framework of thought, which presumably includes the mind's basic concepts or categories (1967: 86–7). Given the plurality of languages, there must be many world pictures or frameworks for understanding reality; and these must be changeable, since language is part of a culture, and culture changes.

Hayek leaves very much in doubt the possibility that reason, linked as it is to the evolution of mind and civilisation, can ever achieve a view of reality that has a justifiable claim to finality. Such a view would seem to be impossible from within the historical process; and if history has no end, there would appear to be no final or privileged standpoint that would permit reason to grasp timeless principles. One must wonder, however, if such a teaching can accommodate Hayek's own ambitious programme, which puts forward a synoptic view of mind, civilization, order and liberty with a considerable degree of finality.

Values

The concept of 'values' is pivotal to Hayek's overall account of knowledge and to his defence of freedom. Later we will see that Hayek's 'ideal' embodies a very specific set of values. In this section I want to make three points. First, Hayek rejected the fact–value dichotomy, even when it was widely accepted by social scientists. Second, Hayek understands values in terms of rules to be followed rather than as particular ends to be pursued by the rational will. Third, Hayek would become increasingly concerned with the sources of values and would look to his theory of social evolution to identify these sources.

(1) As for the fact–value dichotomy, Hayek denies that sense data, particularly as defined by natural science, constitute meaningful facts. In the 1940s, he had undertaken to show that the social sciences cannot possibly succeed in their task of understanding social reality if they limit themselves to facts as defined by natural science: 'our data must be man and the physical world as they appear to men whose actions we try to explain' (1952b [1979]: 60). Hayek here emphasises that the facts of the social sciences are merely 'beliefs or opinions held by particular people ... irrespective of whether they are true or false' (ibid.: 47).

The important point to note here is that people's ordinary beliefs and opinions about the world – the starting point for social science – are suffused with values. The facts of the social sciences are inseparable from values, and social inquiry cannot abstract from them, as natural science attempts to do. In *The Constitution of Liberty*, as in these earlier writings, Hayek emphasises the centrality of values to all social life. He would continue decades later to insist that values are 'the indispensable foundation of all our civilization,' including all our efforts at rational construction and science (1973: 6–7).

(2) Hayek's reservations about theories of action that centre on the exercise of will and on means/ends calculation are more or less implicit in *The Constitution of Liberty*, but they are developed elsewhere. In sum, he associates such theories with constructivist rationalism, inasmuch as they 'attempt to assess an action by its foreseeable results in the particular case,' based on what is presumed to be an 'incontrovertible knowledge of cause and effect.' From the rationalist standpoint, values are understood as

'the concrete ends which determine [the individual's] actions at particular moments.' Projecting into the future and drawing on its presumed knowledge of cause and effect, the rational will supposedly deduces the best means of achieving the desired end.

Hayek, by contrast, denies the will's autonomy and subordinates it to habit. Values are not particular concrete ends, but general rules that are embodied in tradition and opinion. These rules, derived from countless centuries of human experience, tell us what is permissible or impermissible insofar as action is concerned. They 'confine our actions to the limited range within which we are able to foresee relevant consequences' and also prevent us 'from overstepping these limits.' In fact, it is because of such boundaries that our causal knowledge about the likely consequences of a particular course of action can serve us effectively. These rules enable the individual actor, when caught up in the emotions of the moment, 'to avoid actions of a kind whose foreseeable results seemed desirable, but which were likely to lead to the destruction of the order on which the achievements of the human race rested' (see 1978a: 82–8).

(3) As we see, values are indispensable to action, but where do they come from? Hayek insists on the 'givenness of the value framework,' by which he means that each of us is born into some system of values – one that 'supplies the end which our reason must serve.' When Hayek declares that we 'must always work inside a framework of both values and institutions which is not of our own making,' he is referring to an evolving framework and not to one that reflects absolute eternal values (63). So long as reason remains within this given framework, it can provide useful clarifications and also formulate rules or laws that implement sound values, but it cannot be the originating source of

values. Rationalism's hope of replacing tradition with a 'deliberately constructed, synthetic system of morals' is destined to fail (65).

Even though some particular value framework is 'given' for each society, Hayek, in his theory of social evolution, does look behind this 'givenness' for the primary sources of all values. Values are general rules, and these may arise from man's biological instincts, from cumulative experience and from conscious articulation. Instinctive values predominate in the earliest societies, while the conscious articulation of values comes about only with the advent of civilisation. Traditions in the strict sense – those rules that arise from cumulative experience and are followed habitually and unconsciously – develop in society from the beginning and cannot be replaced by rules or laws that people frame deliberately (see Hayek's 1978 Hobhouse Lecture, 'The Three Sources of Human Values,' which appears as an epilogue to the third volume of *Law, Legislation and Liberty* [1979]).

Hayek employs this framework to explain the modern discontent with civilisation and to criticise socialism. Instinctive values, which emphasised sharing, care for one's neighbours, and sacrifice for the common good, were suited for sustaining very small communities. With the advent of urban life and civilisation, traditions and rules evolved that favoured a large and impersonal extended order, or commercial society. The problem is that 'in some respects man's biological equipment has not kept pace with that rapid change, that the adaptation of his non-rational part has lagged somewhat, and that many of his instincts and emotions are still more adapted to the life of a hunter than to life in civilization.' This maladaptation has given rise to an instinctive dissatisfaction with civilised life – the sense that it is 'unnatural' – and to all 'the familiar complaints against industrialism, capitalism, or overre-finement' (40).

Hayek wants to underscore the indispensability of habitual or customary rules for the kind of civilisation that we now enjoy. Strictly speaking, the term 'tradition' refers to rules of this kind. Hayek acknowledges, of course, that deliberately articulated rules are indispensable to the progress of modern civilisation – the Rule of Law attests to that – but these are not to be understood as novel constructions. Their continuity with rules that have evolved through trial and error over a long period of time is crucial to their effectiveness.

Hayek's distinction between three kinds of values (instinctive, traditional, articulated) ties in closely with his critique of socialism. A free society rests on tradition-based values, but these are jeopardised both by our instinctual promptings and by rationalist ambitions. Socialism, in Hayek's view, exemplifies both dangers. On the one hand, socialists cast tradition aside and prefer constructed rules to ones that have evolved. On the other hand, socialism is 'an atavism,' i.e. it wants to re-establish society on instinct-based values such as solidarity and social justice. Socialism is a form of primitivism. It is fundamentally at odds with those values that make possible large societies, civilisation and human freedom (1976: 143–50; 1978a: 57–68; 1979: 165–76; 1988: 11–37). It is an enemy of the extended, rule-governed, open society, or what Hayek, in *Law, Legislation and Liberty*, calls 'the Great Society' (1973: 2; 1976: 107–13; 1988: 19–21, 104).

Moral rules

The most important values, for Hayek, are the general rules

embodied in a society's traditions and beliefs as well as in man's own unconscious habits. Within the totality of such rules or values, Hayek distinguishes moral values from the rest. Moral values are rules of social conduct; and Hayek insists that we have 'no choice but to submit' to such rules, even though we might not know the rationale for them or see 'that anything important depends on their being observed in the particular instance.' Moral rules address us as unconditional demands and not as expedient options: 'At any one stage of our evolution, the system of values into which we are born supplies the ends which our reason must serve.' Moral rules thus resemble Kant's categorical imperative, but of course they are products of social evolution and not formulations of the rational will. Even Kantian ethics is derivative from a prior tradition, i.e. it is an extension of 'the basic idea underlying the rule of law' (62–6; 196–7).

Insofar as possible, Hayek wants to make tradition and moral rules self-legitimising. The alternative – to have their legitimacy dependent on something else – is both unattractive to him and contrary to his understanding of moral experience. He could, for example, argue that we ought to obey traditional rules because in doing so we promote a larger end. This would, however, require the everyday actor to think like a social theorist. As Hayek writes later, 'acting individuals usually do not understand' the 'functions' of cultural rules that emerge spontaneously (1979: 155). A social theorist such as Hayek does take an instrumentalist view, because he sees that obedience to moral rules produces spontaneous order and also determines whether an evolving society will survive and prosper in the long run. The theorist recognises that 'the ultimate decision about what is good or bad will be made not by individual human wisdom but by the decline of the groups that have adhered to the "wrong" beliefs' (35–6). Social actors, however, perceive moral rules as 'a value in itself' and do not require instrumentalist or expedient reasons for obeying them.

Another way to legitimise traditional rules would be to seek support from religion, but Hayek, as a scientist, had refused throughout his career to take this path. He rejects all causal explanations that appeal to invisible essences or hidden spiritual forces, since these amount to superstition. Nevertheless, he concedes that there are 'good reasons why any person who wants to live and act successfully in society must accept many common beliefs, though the value of these reasons may have little to do with their demonstrative truth.' This requirement 'applies to all our values,' but 'it is most important in the case of moral rules of conduct' (64–5).

In this guarded and even cryptic statement, Hayek is silent as to whether these 'common beliefs' have a religious character and whether they might serve to legitimise the moral rules to which they are attached. Much later, in *The Fatal Conceit*, Hayek addresses these issues directly. He wonders whether he has underestimated the role of religious belief in sustaining beneficial customs: 'even an agnostic ought to concede that we owe our morals, and the tradition that has provided not only our civilization but our very lives, to the acceptance of' claims that are scientifically unacceptable, such as those advanced by religion' (1988: 137). In an appendix, he cites favourably Sir James Frazer's argument that superstition rendered humanity a great service by protecting marriage and private property (ibid.: 157). Of course, traditional rules cannot be self-legitimising if they must depend on the authority of religion (or superstition) to uphold their authority.

Hayek seeks not only to describe the role that values play in social life, but above all to justify a particular set of values, as portrayed in his 'ideal.' Later I will consider Hayek's ideal and its foundations, but now we must sum up what we learn about moral obligation from his discussion of values.

Ordinary morality is based on an unquestioned imperative to obey established rules, but this is not Hayek's last word on moral obligation as such. First of all, it leaves no room for novelty, which is essential to the progress of civilisation. Often it is desirable that the individual should be able to transgress established moral rules – voluntary ones and not those imposed coercively by the state – 'when it seems to him worthwhile to incur the odium which this will cause.' Furthermore, the social pressure enforcing these rules should be variable, so as to 'allow for gradual and experimental change' (63). Where individuals and groups simultaneously observe partially different rules, there is a greater opportunity 'for the selection of the more effective ones' (63). Such flexibility makes gradual evolution and spontaneous growth possible and permits modification and improvements in light of new experience (63). Clearly civilised life is marked by a tension between the traditional and the novel. A question left open here is the source of the innovator's values.

Taking the long view, Hayek insists that a process of selection is at work in society's evolution, winnowing out moral rules that might be destructive to society and preserving those that favour its survival or persistence. Sometimes he speaks of broader achievements, such as 'success,' but he stops well short of Nietzsche's idea that every people creates and honours those values that make them 'rule and triumph and shine, to the awe and envy of their neighbors' (Nietzsche, 1954: 170). For Hayek, the will to survive, and not the will to power, drives the evolutionary process.

Hayek's moral principles are no derivative from evolutionary theory. Individuals cannot possibly be under an imperative to follow moral rules that will, in the long run, ensure society's survival or success, since the future is unpredictable. Only rarely can we know what the eventual results of our actions will be. Even when a group or nation follows the teachings of what it regards as its best men, it may 'destroy itself by the moral beliefs to which it adheres.' When it comes to the values that preserve society, these are selected by an impersonal evolutionary process and not by far-sighted individuals. Imagining that we can foresee or plan the future is a rationalistic illusion. The best we can do is to maintain a free society, where individuals can choose among competing ideals, and to cultivate diverse human capacities. In such a society, destructive tendencies are 'self-corrective,' since 'groups guided by "impractical" ideals would decline, and others, less moral by current standards, would take their place' (67).

I close on a cautionary note. Hayek provides two separate and somewhat different accounts of value in *The Constitution of Liberty*. The first account – the one that we have just now explored – is developed chiefly in Chapter 4, in connection with the discussion of tradition, moral rules and opinion. Here Hayek emphasises that moral rules typically demand unconditional obedience from the individual and that social pressure to conform to moral rules is both potent and beneficial. The second discussion of value comes in Chapter 6, in connection with a discussion of justice and its relation to economics. Here Hayek insists that society values the 'results' of the individual's actions more than his moral merit, implying some relaxation in conformist pressures. The two discussions differ in tone, if not in substance, although both strongly defend freedom of action. Whether their discussions of values and moral rules can be reconciled remains to be seen.

4 EQUALITY, FREEDOM AND JUST DISTRIBUTION (CHAPTERS 4, 6 AND 8)

Chapter 6, 'Equality, Value, and Merit,' is essentially about justice, even though the chapter's title and organisation fail to make this clear. To understand the chapter's central argument, it helps to distinguish, as Hayek himself does, between distributive and commutative justice (440–41, n. 10 and n. 11; cf. 232). As Hayek notes, this distinction among kinds of justice goes back to Aristotle and the Greeks. Commutative justice is concerned principally with agreements or contracts among private individuals and their proper enforcement. Distributive justice involves the distribution of the community's goods by those who have authority over those goods.

Chapter 6 is concerned with distributive justice, and Hayek's aim is to discredit the idea that it should be the organising principle of society. Hayek will argue that neither human equality nor human merit is a proper basis for distributing the community's goods. In fact, government has no business deciding how wealth should be distributed among individuals. Of course, wealth does somehow get distributed, and Hayek must provide an alternative to distribution by government. His solution is to rely on economic freedom and the market. The market distributes goods according to the 'value' of individuals and not according to principles of equality and merit. This argument requires, however, that Hayek define value in such a way that it does not mean moral merit, in the sense discussed in Chapter 4.

Are individuals equal?

Hayek's critique of egalitarianism begins by affirming a kind of equality: 'The great aim of the struggle for liberty has been equality before the law.' Law is here understood to include two kinds of general rules: those enforced by the state and those bearing on moral and social conduct that we obey voluntarily. Liberty requires the equal application of both kinds of rules. The equality of state-enforced rules is discussed later in connection with the Rule of Law. As for equal rules of moral and social conduct, Hayek has in mind what Tocqueville called the manners or mores of democratic society, as distinguished from those of an aristocracy (see Tocqueville, 2000: 45–53, 535–41). Democratic manners require that individuals relate to each other as equals and not in terms of social rank or status.

This equality of the general rules of law and conduct is, in Hayek's estimation, 'the only kind of equality conducive to liberty and the only equality which we can secure without destroying liberty' (85). One might think that equality before the law presupposes an underlying equality of some sort among individuals to whom the law applies, but Hayek seems to deny that this is the case: if we are to understand the meaning of equality before the law, 'the first requirement is that we free ourselves from the belief in factual equality' (87). '[T]he factual equality of all men' is obviously an 'untrue ... assumption' (86). What Hayek means by 'factual equality' is unclear, but at least it includes the belief that 'all men are born equal' (87). In dismissing this tenet as factually untrue, Hayek rejects a key principle of early liberalism, whose case for equality before the law was grounded in natural rights that individuals are born with and possess equally as human beings.

The relevant fact about human beings is not equality but difference: 'It is of the essence of the demand for equality before the law that people should be treated alike in spite of the fact that they are different' (86). By 'difference,' Hayek means primarily the inequalities among people that arise from both 'nature' and 'nurture.' Nature does not make individuals equal, but it does make them unequal in capacities, talents and such. As for nurture, social life, especially the family, produces inequalities that give some individuals an advantage over others.

We must pause to wonder whether Hayek's case for freedom doesn't require a natural or inherent equality among individuals and whether, in repudiating this idea, he jeopardises his own position.

First, the very idea of 'the individual' – the human being shorn of all qualities that make him different from others – is an egalitarian concept, especially when it is interpreted to mean that each individual should enjoy equal freedom in his own private sphere. Second, Hayek builds his case for freedom on the principle that each individual should be free to pursue his own aims or plan of life. If another forces me to submit to his will, he is using me as a means to his end and thus is violating my freedom: 'Coercion is evil precisely because it thus eliminates an individual as a thinking and valuing person and makes him a bare tool in the achievement of the ends of another' (21).

This argument requires a moral imperative of the kind that Kant articulated – namely, that human beings must always be treated as an end and not merely as a means to someone else's purposes. At one point Hayek writes: 'A society that does not recognize that each individual has values of his own which he is entitled to follow can have no respect for the dignity of the individual and cannot really know freedom' (79). Where does this individual entitlement to one's own values come from, and why is it true that individuals as such have a 'dignity' that we must respect? We are touching here on Hayek's ultimate justification for freedom. He is mostly silent on the matter, apparently because of a reluctance to acknowledge that human beings are in some fundamental ways inherently equal.

While some aspects of democratic society are disturbing to Hayek, he speaks favourably of egalitarian manners: The 'extension of the principle of equality to the rules of moral and social conduct is the chief expression of what is commonly called the democratic spirit – and probably that aspect of it that does most to make inoffensive the inequalities that liberty necessarily produces' (85). By the same token, Hayek opposes social arrangements based on class privilege and extreme differences in wealth:

> One may well feel attracted to a community in which there are no extreme contrasts between rich and poor and may welcome the fact that the general increase in wealth seems gradually to reduce these differences. I fully share these feelings and certainly regard the degree of social equality that the United States has achieved as wholly admirable. (87–8)

One might favour 'more even or more just distribution' while rejecting coercive means to bring this about. Indeed, social equality can be a valid policy consideration: 'Wherever there is a legitimate need for government action and we have to choose between different methods of satisfying such a need, those that incidentally also reduce inequality may well be preferable.' For example, the law of intestate succession might be so framed as to favour equality. Lest he be misunderstood, Hayek concludes these remarks by emphasising once again that coercion should not to be used to bring about substantive equality (87–8).

Hayek clearly prefers what Tocqueville called a democratic social condition to an aristocratic one, although like Tocqueville he would insist that this condition exhibit the principle of free competition rather than the spirit of envy. Clearly he wants to avoid a society polarised between the wealthy and the poor. This means encouraging a broad middle class, which has sufficient wealth to look out for itself and avoid dependency on government. One basis for his opposition to inflationary policies is that they devalue savings and tend to destroy the middle class (see 338).

Inequality, law and freedom

Individuals differ from each other because of inherent and acquired qualities that make them unequal. These inequalities, and the advantages they convey, should be protected by legal and customary rules. Hayek opposes efforts to neutralise them by coercive means, whether to provide 'equality of opportunity' or to assure substantively equal outcomes. Such actions violate 'the basic postulate of a free society, namely, the limitation of all coercion by equal law.' Moreover, they would require a weighing of human potentialities; but no man or group of men has such a capacity, and certainly no one should be trusted invariably to exercise it (88). In a free society, 'economic inequality is not one of the evils which justify our resorting to discriminatory coercion or privilege as a remedy' (87–8).

Equality before the law not only protects inequality, but – by freeing individuals to use their talents and industry to gain their own ends – increases it. As Hayek observes, the 'equality before the law which freedom requires leads to material inequality.' Again, liberty is 'bound to produce inequality in many respects' (87, 85).

Hayek recognises that a defence of liberty requires some justification for the advantages that it permits some people to enjoy. One approach would be to show that liberty serves the good of individuals by allowing those who are talented and enterprising to get ahead. Hayek does make such an argument in *The Constitution of Liberty*, but here he emphasises how society itself benefits from this inequality. He argues, for example, that the inequality resulting from individual liberty provides society with valuable information. It demonstrates 'that some manners of living are more successful than others' (85). Another point is that 'the acquisition by any member of the community of additional capacities to do things which may be valuable must always be regarded as a gain for that community' (88). Indeed, 'society is likely to get a better elite' if some fortunate individuals are able to acquire valuable qualities through family nurture and inheritance (90).

From Hayek's standpoint, any coercive action by the state to assure equality of outcomes is a violation of individual liberty. The same is true of coercive efforts to secure 'equality of opportunity.' Hayek defends several institutions – the family, rules of inheritance, education – against egalitarian demands to reform them for the sake of equal opportunity. In each case he argues that society benefits when each member starts with as many advantages as possible.

It is important to note that Hayek is not opposed to equal opportunity as such, but only to certain egalitarian applications of this principle. He points out that classical liberalism, at its height, had demanded 'that all man-made obstacles to the rise of some should be removed, that all privileges of individuals should be abolished, and that what the state contributed to the chance of improving one's conditions should be the same for all.' Liberals had held that 'all should be allowed to try,' but recognised that individual differences will give some an advantage over others. The more recent view – the one that Hayek opposes – insists that 'all must be assured an equal start and the same prospects.' This approach requires governmental intervention and adjustments that curb individual freedom (92–3). Hayek strongly defends the older understanding of opportunity:

> Let us by all means endeavor to increase opportunities for all. But we ought to do so in the full knowledge that to increase opportunities for all is likely to favor those better able to take advantage of them and may often at first increase inequalities. Where the demand for 'equality of opportunity' leads to attempts to eliminate such 'unfair advantages,' it is only likely to do harm. All human differences, whether they are differences in natural gifts or in opportunities, create unfair advantages. But, since the chief contribution of any individual is to make the best use of the accidents he encounters, success must to a great extent be a matter of chance. (388)

Benefits of inequality

Hayek offers a justification for inequality in several places in *The Constitution of Liberty*. In Chapter 3, he provides a spirited defence of inequality as indispensable to civilisation's progress. Since a rising standard of life depends more on an increase in knowledge than on the accumulation of capital, one might expect Hayek to defend primarily the scientists or inventors who lead the way in discovering useful knowledge. Here, however, he defends the position of the rich, whose way of life contributes a kind of unintended knowledge that is indispensable to progress. Their contribution is to experiment 'with a style of living that will eventually be available to many.' Hayek avoids any distinction here between legitimate and illegitimate wealth, regardless of its source, amount or use. The rich teach the rest, but inadvertently and by example rather than by purposeful instruction.

To defend inequalities of wealth, Hayek contends that '[t]here is no way of making generally accessible new and still expensive ways of living except by their being initially practiced by some.' Thus 'in any phase of progress the rich, by experimenting with new styles of living not yet accessible to the poor, perform a necessary service without which the advance of the poor would be very much slower.' As the poor seek to imitate the lifestyle of the rich, the cost of producing new goods comes down, so that eventually they become affordable to many. Indeed, '[e]ven the poorest today owe their relative material well-being to the results of past inequality.' Meanwhile, the rich are beginning to enjoy new goods that will be sought by the masses some decades hence. Hayek insists that his is a valid argument and not some 'far-fetched and cynical apologetics.' Even so, he concedes that it will not assuage those who fail to achieve the desired results or feel 'the pain of unfulfilled desire aroused by the example of others' (44–5). This of course gives rise to problems of justice and envy in democratic societies.

Hayek goes on to apply this argument to the international scene, holding that the poor nations learn much from the rich ones and, by aspiring to imitate them, contribute both to their own progress and to that of civilisation. His key point here is that the advantage of the West is due mainly to its 'more effective utilization of knowledge' and not to 'a greater accumulation of capital.' This knowledge has cost the leading nations much to obtain, but it is a 'free gift' to those who follow, enabling them 'to reach the same level at a much smaller cost' (46–7).

In Chapter 8, Hayek makes a case for 'the man of independent means' and for entrepreneurs in particular. He points out that in modern democratic society, 'most of us work as employed members of large organizations, using resources we do not own and acting largely on the instructions given by others' (118). The principles of freedom were developed, however, in a society where most people, and particularly the influential ones, 'were independent in the activities that gave them their livelihood.' The question is whether the interests and outlook of employed persons are supportive of a free society. Hayek thinks that the fact of being employed not only affects a person's 'initiative and inventiveness,' but also greatly limits his knowledge 'of the responsibilities of those who control resources,' including the allocation of capital (122). Moreover, people tend to choose employment, rather than independence, because they 'want the relative security and absence of risk, and responsibility that an employed position brings,' or because they expect that employment will offer a larger income and a more satisfying activity (120). The employee is likely to think that his income should depend on his merit, not on the results of his initiatives.

These developments have had a great impact on modern politics. Not surprisingly, the employed prefer a paternalistic government, a 'higher tutelary power' that will provide a broad range of social services and oversee 'the directing activities which they do not understand but on which their livelihood depends'

(123). They are attracted to the idea that the state, in taxing and in providing services, should aim for social justice. They come to regard persons who make their living by employing capital as a privileged class or special interest 'which can justly be discriminated against' (123). Little do they realise that their own opportunities for employment ultimately depend on 'the existence of independent individuals who can take the initiative in the continuous process of re-forming and redirecting organizations' (124).

Men of independent means are essential to preserving competitive enterprise, but their most important contribution to a free society is the leadership they provide, especially 'in the field of cultural amenities, in the fine arts, in education and research, in the preservation of natural beauty and historic treasures, and above all, in the propagation of new ideas in politics, morals, and religion' (125). From this standpoint Hayek defends not only entrepreneurs, but also a leisured class, whose members likely will have grown up to appreciate non-material goods and also to feel an obligation to take the lead in intellectual, moral and artistic affairs. In most of the USA, this class has almost completely disappeared, so that businessmen now lack intellectual leadership and have no 'coherent and defensible philosophy of life.' A progressive society requires 'a cultural elite within the propertied class' (128–9).

Merit and value

Hayek's underlying concern in Chapter 6 is the problem of distributive justice. Already he has shown that government must not, as a matter of law, distribute goods to persons according to the principle of equality. This leaves open, however, the possibility that unequal distributions may be warranted. Hayek knew of the important tradition in moral philosophy which holds that unequal distributions are just if they are based on the relative merit of the recipients. To complete his case against state-sponsored distributive justice, Hayek must now rule out the option of distributing material goods according to personal merit. This leads him to draw a crucial distinction between 'merit' and 'value.'

In Chapter 4, Hayek had described the meritorious person as one who complies with established moral rules. Society pressures individuals to behave morally and it praises or blames them, depending on whether or not they do so. Hayek writes: 'How we value another person will necessarily depend on what his values are' (79). In Chapter 6, however, he argues that we mostly leave morality aside in valuing other persons and look primarily at the results of their actions. Looking at both chapters together, we see that Hayek uses the term 'value' in a generic sense to include both value as merit and value as results: 'Though moral value or merit is a species of value, not all value is moral value, and most of our judgments of value are not moral judgments' (98).

Hayek's distinction between merit and value can be illustrated by an example. Suppose that someone has acted with a view to achieving a result. Value is to be found in the action's results, as assessed by others. Merit, by contrast, is an attribute of the actor's conduct – namely, the moral attribute that makes the conduct worthy of praise. Merit is disconnected from whether or not an action achieves its intended result. It lies in the actor's 'subjective effort' and not in the action's 'objective outcome.' Conduct can thus be meritorious even if unsuccessful and thus lacking in value. By the same token, successful conduct can be valuable, even though it lacks merit (94–5).

Merit, as Hayek describes it, rests on two conditions: the actor must do 'what some accepted rule of conduct' demands of him; and the action must have 'cost him some pain and effort.' By making merit relative to variable rules of conduct, Hayek turns away from traditional moral philosophy, which typically had sought a single standard of merit by referring to human nature. Hayek's second condition – that meritorious action requires some pain and effort – implies such a standard, but unlike traditional thinkers, he takes this requirement as a reason to belittle striving for merit: 'The fact is, of course, that we do not wish people to earn a maximum of merit but to achieve a maximum of usefulness at a minimum of pain and sacrifice and therefore a minimum of merit' (96). Hayek illustrates this point with the example of an accomplished surgeon who is able to achieve a good result with ease, because of many years of arduous practice: 'we feel that we are doing justice if we recompense value rendered with equal value, without inquiring what it might have cost the particular individual to supply us with these services' (97). By separating value from merit, Hayek implies that one should follow the convenient path, which is usefulness to others at little cost to oneself, and not the arduous path of moral virtue (see 81–3).

Making material rewards conform to merit might be feasible for an organisation, but this is both impracticable and undesirable for society at large. Basing rewards on merit would require a determination of each individual's 'subjective effort,' including the use made of opportunities and the degree of effort and self-denial. Even in the unlikely event that such determinations were successful, the results would be incompatible with a free society. Everyone's success would require that others approve their moral conduct, thus injuring disfavoured groups and reducing the incentive for individuals to pursue the outcomes that they think best. Moreover, some authority would have to assign rewards for merit.

Value is assigned not by central authority but by the market: 'The market will generally offer for services of any kind the value they will have for those who benefit from them' (96). Market-based rewards stimulate individual efforts and extend economic freedom to productive groups that might lack general approval for their conduct. Judgements of individual merit are subjective, but value is an 'objective outcome,' based on the results of one's actions and dispersed assessments of their benefits. Since the market generally assures that value is rewarded, government's role is primarily to facilitate market distributions by maintaining the rule of law. Certainly it has no business pursuing social justice (96–100; cf. 80–83).

5 MAJORITY RULE AND LIMITED GOVERNMENT (CHAPTERS 7 AND 10)

The problem of reconciling liberalism with democracy is one of Hayek's chief concerns in *The Constitution of Liberty*. The problem is this: liberalism is a doctrine about human liberty or freedom and how to protect and extend it by setting limits to government. Democracy, as understood by many theorists and as often practised, subordinates liberty to the quest for equality. Can liberty flourish where the people are sovereign and the will of the majority prevails? Hayek turns now to the question of majority rule and its limits.

Majority rule and the community

Democratic government can be structured in different ways, and Hayek is quite vague here as to the kind of arrangement that he chiefly has in mind. The idea of majority rule presupposes some collectivity within which this rule takes place. Any group, of course, can entrust decision-making authority to a majority of its members; but not every group or collectivity is decisive for political life. Hayek has different ways of identifying the politically relevant group – state, country, society – but the one he settles on is 'the community.' As we get deeper into *The Constitution of Liberty*, it becomes clear that Hayek assigns vast powers to the community and gives it a surprisingly important role in political life.

Hayek explains that 'the authority of democratic decision rests on its being made by the majority of a community which is held together by certain beliefs common to most members.' Indeed, 'it is the acceptance of such common principles that makes a collection of people a community.' Hayek goes on to insist that majority rule must be consistent with the community's common beliefs or principles and cannot override them: 'it is necessary that the majority submit to these common principles even when it may be in its immediate interest to violate them.' The key point is that 'the power of the majority is limited by those commonly held principles and that there is no legitimate power beyond them' (106–7).

This formulation raises two problems that we must consider. First, in what sense does 'the majority of a community' make the authoritative decisions in a democracy? Second, does it make a difference what opinions or beliefs a community holds?

Various seventeenth-century doctrines of community lie in the background of Hayek's political thought, especially those deriving from Locke and from Rousseau. For Locke, individuals form a particular commonwealth when they leave the state of nature, to be governed 'by such Rules as the Community, or those authorized by them to that purpose, shall agree on' (*Second Treatise*, no. 127). The community, by the consent of the majority, entrusts power to a government, which provides for 'establish'd *standing Laws*, promulgated and known to the People;' for '*indifferent* and upright *Judges*,' who will decide controversies by those laws; and for a power that will execute those laws at home and secure the community against foreign invasion (no. 131). The majority of the community, which has 'the whole power of the Community, naturally in them,' may choose among several forms of government. It may decide to itself 'imploy all that power in making

Laws for the Community from time to time, and Executing those Laws by Officers of their own appointing.' In this case, 'the *Form* of the Government is a perfect *Democracy*.' The majority may, however, choose from other forms: an oligarchy, consisting of 'a few select Men, and their Heirs or Successors;' a monarchy, either hereditary or elected; or some mixed form of government that is compounded from these (no. 132). The point is that majority rule may occur at either of two levels: the majority's decision as to the form of government (which need not be a democracy); and the majority's exercise of political power (if it decides to institute a democratic form).

Rousseau's innovation is to insist that the community must retain the lawmaking power and not delegate it to others. What can be delegated is only the power of government or the executive power (see *On the Social Contract*, II: 1–6). Like Rousseau, Hayek distinguishes sharply between lawmaking and governing. He also commends Rousseau for understanding that the laws must always be general in form (194; also Hayek, 1992: 251–2). Hayek is highly critical, however, of other teachings of Rousseau, including his insistence that law is an act of will by the community (Hayek, 1973: 25; cf. 1976: 147).

More recent majoritarian conceptions of democracy offer still another way to understand majority rule. Unlike Rousseau, these conceptions assign legislative power to a representative legislature, but hold that the elected representatives should enact the specific policies favoured by a majority of the community. The people's representatives make the law (presumably by a majority vote), but the law's direction is determined by majority opinion in the community.

In Hayek's case, one must decide whether he is speaking

of majority rule by the community or by a legislative body. The liberal and the democratic traditions agree that 'whenever state action is required, and particularly whenever coercive rules have to be laid down, the decision ought to be made by the majority' (106). Hayek accepts this requirement, but it does not specify the level or levels at which majority rule should occur. In the present chapter, Hayek seems mostly to have in mind the formation of majority opinion within community itself, which will then 'guide' or 'direct' the actions of government (109). Implicitly he takes the view that community opinion, as determined by the majority, is binding on government.

Limited and arbitrary government

The liberal tradition, following ancient writers, had identified several alternative forms of government. The ancients taught that these forms differ fundamentally from each other, since they empower different types of human beings; and their primary concern was to decide which form is best in itself as well as best under given conditions. With the advent of liberalism, attention shifted from essential or qualitative differences among the forms of rule to what all governments chiefly have in common, namely a quantity of power and a tendency to abuse it. The urgent problem became one of making government safe by limiting its power; and the key distinction came to be one between 'limited' and 'arbitrary' government. The alternative forms of rule were now seen in this light. Since all governments, if unchecked, endanger freedom, liberals were inclined to think in terms of the least bad form of government rather than the best form.

Hayek follows the liberal tradition in these respects. He

classifies governments mainly according to whether they are limited or arbitrary, so the form of rule becomes a secondary consideration: 'It is not who governs but what government is entitled to do that seems to me to be the essential problem' (403). By limited government, Hayek understands one in which the use of coercive power is constrained by general rules that are well established and effective. By arbitrary government, he understands political rule that is not constrained by law. Arbitrary government, in all of its forms, endangers liberty.

Democracy versus elite rule

Insofar as the various forms of rule are concerned, Hayek distinguishes mainly between government by the few, or elite rule, and government by the many, or majority rule. He subsumes both alternatives – elite rule and majority rule – under his primary distinction between 'limited' and 'arbitrary.' This means that there can be limited governments of either an elite or a democratic form. Alternatively there can be arbitrary governments of either form. Thus, for example, elite rule can be a limited government, while democratic rule can be of the arbitrary type. The key question is whether the ruling body subordinates itself to the law.

The desirability of elite rule obviously depends on the qualities of this select group. In line with the liberal tradition, Hayek rejects claims to power based merely on an advantageous birth or on superior wealth. The only kind of elite rule worthy of consideration is that of 'the wisest and best informed.' Hayek grants the possibility that 'in any given state of affairs, government by some educated elite would be a more efficient and perhaps even more just government than one chosen by majority vote' (108). Even so, he concludes that 'democracy is probably the best form of limited government' or, stated more cautiously, that majority rule is perhaps 'the least evil of those forms of government from which we have to choose' (116, 403).

Hayek identifies 'three chief arguments by which democracy can be justified, each of which may be regarded as conclusive.' First, counting numbers is less wasteful than fighting in determining which among conflicting opinions has the stronger support: 'Democracy is the only method of peaceful change that man has yet discovered.' A second argument – very important historically though perhaps not always valid now – is that 'the prospects of individual liberty are better in a democracy than under other forms of government.' This is because democracy fosters certain qualities, such as courage and industry, which inspire and safeguard individual liberty. Also, 'since coercive power must in fact always be exercised by a few,' its abuse is less likely if it can be revoked by the many who must submit to it. A third argument – in Hayek's view the most powerful one – is that democratic institutions improve 'the general level of understanding of public affairs.' What Hayek has chiefly in mind here is the way majority opinion is formed through debate among contending views. Democratic opinion is not static, but grows out of a dynamic process that favours the progress of knowledge. Hayek can thus agree with Tocqueville that 'democracy is the only effective method of educating the majority.' Also, when knowledge is diffused broadly, a wide range of persons is available from which to select those who will govern (107–9).

Democracy is a procedure only

Limiting the popular majority is a pressing concern for Hayek; and his solution is tied up with his insistence that democracy is only a method or procedure for reaching decisions, with no fixed aims of its own. As we have seen, Hayek regards majority rule as the safest and most successful way for the community to reach important decisions, and he defends democracy on this basis alone. Democracy is a means and not an end in itself. It is a method or procedure for deciding on common ends, but it has no ends of its own (106; cf. 109). Democracy as such 'indicates nothing about the aims of government' (104). This means that liberals and democrats are both wrong in connecting democracy to a substantive end: i.e. to freedom or to equality.

What Hayek says about majority rule in the community must be seen in this light. Hayek requires that majority rule be consistent with the community's common beliefs or principles, but initially at least he leaves open the content of those beliefs or principles. From this standpoint, it would seem that democracy is consistent with fascism or with what J. L. Talmon has called 'totalitarian democracy' (56), if this is what the community believes in. Certainly it is consistent with socialism: 'when the opinion of the community decides what different people shall receive, the same authority must also decide what they shall do' (232).

Detaching democracy from fixed ends or principles opens the door to oppression; and Hayek offers two ways around this problem. One solution is to require that majority decisions take the form of general rules: 'So long as democracy constrains the individual only by general rules of its own making, it controls the power of coercion' (116). It is dangerous for democracy to go beyond this and specify ends to be achieved, since this will extend the discretionary power of the administrators. Thus the individual 'has little reason to fear any general laws which the majority may pass, but he has much reason to fear the rulers it may put over him to implement its direction' (116). Under this solution, constraining government by general rules or laws is sufficient to protect freedom, regardless of the opinions or beliefs that are held by the community and voiced by the majority.

Hayek does, however, offer an alternative solution, which is to instil beliefs or opinions that are favourable to liberty. One may profoundly respect the convention that the majority view should prevail in collective action, 'but this does not in the least mean that one should not make every effort to alter it' (109). Hayek follows this with a very long discussion (considered earlier) of how opinion comes to be formed in democratic communities and especially how the ideas of theorists or political philosophers influence public opinion in the long run. Making democracy safe for liberty is primarily an educational task: 'democracy has yet to learn that, in order to be just, it must be guided in its action by general principles' (314). Hayek undertakes to supply these principles through his teaching on the Rule of Law and limited government. *The Constitution of Liberty* is an educational enterprise, designed to shape belief and opinion in a democratic age.

Hayek is much more favourable to democracy in *The Constitution of Liberty* than in *Law, Legislation and Liberty*. In the former, he attributes democracy's excesses mostly to a lack of understanding, the solution to which is education or enlightenment. Later Hayek came to believe that democracy had devolved into unlimited or arbitrary government and had become something of a game in which government tries to maintain a majority coalition by 'satisfying the demands of a multitude of special interests' (1979: 99; cf.

98–104). This leads him to develop institutional means of limiting majority rule, which he incorporates into a model constitution (ibid.: 105–27).

PART II
FREEDOM AND THE LAW

6 THE RULE OF LAW AND ITS DETRACTORS (CHAPTERS 14 AND 16)

Hayek's primary aim in *The Constitution of Liberty* is to explain the meaning and practical significance of the Rule of Law. Part II, where this ideal is portrayed, is the book's centre, both literally and substantively.

Hayek had often spoken of the Rule of Law in earlier writings (see 1944b [2007b]: 112–23), but his fullest account, prior to *The Constitution of Liberty*, appears in a set of four lectures, delivered in 1955 at the invitation of the Bank of Egypt, entitled *The Political Ideal of the Rule of Law* (1955). Later, Hayek explains that while en route to Egypt, he and his wife spent several months in Europe, retracing a journey that J. S. Mill had once made to Italy and Greece. The trip rekindled Hayek's interest in Mill's *On Liberty* and its case for freedom. The Cairo Lectures, together with his 'constant preoccupation with Mill's thinking,' brought it about that after Hayek returned to Chicago in the autumn of 1955, 'the plan for *The Constitution of Liberty* suddenly stood clearly before my mind ... I had before me a clear plan for a book on liberty arranged round the Cairo lectures' (1994: 129–30). In this light, we see that Part I of *The Constitution of Liberty* takes up questions of individual freedom that Mill wrestled with, but failed to resolve satisfactorily. Part II restates and expands the Cairo Lectures. Part III applies the Rule of Law to issues of government policy. Hayek drew heavily from the Cairo Lectures in preparing *The Constitution of Liberty*; and taking them into account will be helpful in understanding his later exposition.

Importance of the ideal

Deciding what Hayek means by the Rule of Law is a more complex problem than might first appear. 'Rule' here is not to be understood as an activity. Hayek does not mean that the law rules, in the sense of exerting authority over a political community. He is thinking instead of 'rule' as a precept or, more accurately, as an ideal. The Rule of Law depicts what the law should be in a free society. It is a definitive principle or ideal – the ideal of freedom under the law – that stands above and measures the laws of a community. Existing laws, including constitutional provisions as well as ordinary legislation, may approach this ideal, but can never embody it perfectly.

Hayek says this about the importance of having an ideal of liberty:

> Not only is liberty a system under which all government
> action is guided by principles, but it is an ideal that will
> not be preserved unless it is itself accepted as an overriding
> principle governing all particular acts of legislation. Where
> no such fundamental rule is stubbornly adhered to as an
> ultimate ideal about which there must be no compromise
> for the sake of material advantages – as an ideal which, even
> though it may have to be temporarily infringed during a
> passing emergency, must form the basis of all permanent
> arrangements – freedom is almost certain to be destroyed
> by piecemeal encroachments. (68)

The ideal of the Rule of Law is designed to preserve a system of liberty. What remains uncertain, however, is how an ideal as such, as distinct from some particular ideal, is to be understood. What is its cognitive status? Is it grounded in what we can know or experience of reality?

A meta-legal principle

In the Cairo Lectures, Hayek describes the Rule of Law as 'an extra-legal rule' or 'a Meta-Legal principle' (1955: 26, 32–3). Hayek opens Chapter 14 of *The Constitution of Liberty* with a section entitled 'The rule of law [as] a meta-legal doctrine,' and here he quotes the third lecture almost verbatim:

> The rule of law is ... not a rule of the law, but a rule concerning what the law ought to be, a meta-legal doctrine or a political ideal. It will be effective only so far as the legislator feels bound by it. In a democracy this means that it will not prevail unless it forms part of the moral tradition of the community, a common ideal shared and unquestioningly accepted by the majority. (206)

Hayek intends to draw a sharp line between laws and the Rule of Law: 'From the fact that the rule of law is a limitation upon all legislation, it follows that it cannot itself be a law in the same sense as the laws passed by the legislator' (205). Systems of laws or rules are products of the evolutionary process, where man interacts constantly with his environment. The Rule of Law as an ideal or meta-legal principle, while derivative from this process, somehow stands above it as a constant or universal. It provides a standard to which the laws should conform, if they are to remain within bounds. The ideal's political effectiveness will depend on whether a community believes in it, and this depends in turn on that community's moral traditions; but the ideal itself is not reducible to the opinions of a particular community.

Hayek is dealing here with the problem of transcendence, and he had several alternative ways to address it. First, he might have presented the Rule of Law as a 'higher law' or natural law, something timeless that we discover by reasoning on the nature of things. Hayek's Rule of Law can be seen as an up-to-date version of the higher law doctrine, but he rejects natural law. The idea of a constant nature with moral meaning is ruled out by his absorption of reason into civilisation or his understanding of being as process. The Rule of Law does function like the older law of nature, standing above and limiting government; but unlike natural law, it is neutral as regards the ends of human action.

A second alternative was made available by post-Hegelian German historicism. Historicism 'was a school that claimed to recognize necessary laws of historical development and to be able to derive from such insight knowledge of what institutions were appropriate to the existing situation.' It assumed that the mind, by transcending limitations of time and place, can 'explicitly recognize how our present views are determined by circumstances and use this knowledge to remake our institutions in a manner appropriate to our time.' Hayek objects to historicism on two grounds: it leads to an 'extreme relativism,' inasmuch as it posits a separate ideal for each epoch and not a universal ideal for civilisation; and it is 'constructivist,' since it rejects 'all rules that cannot be rationally justified or have not been deliberately designed to achieve a specific purpose' (235–6).

A third alternative was laid out by Max Weber. Weber rejected the historicist claim that there are discoverable laws of history, holding instead that the social scientist is confronted with boundless facts of experience, from which he must select those that will give focus to his research. This selection is achieved by constructing 'ideal types,' which are very different from ideals of a moral or aesthetic character. Ideal types, such as 'capitalism,' are indispensable to social science. While they are designed to study people's values, they rigorously avoid any value judgements of their own or any claim as to what ought to be. Moral and aesthetic ideals have no place in social science, since they have no rational or empirical basis whatever. A scholar may decide to become the advocate for an ideal, but in doing so he leaves science behind and enters the ceaseless conflict that 'rages between different gods.' Weber's 'war of the gods' is his characterisation of the conflict between ideals. The choice among them is ultimately a matter of faith or the individual's subjective decision (Weber, 2004: 17–31; Weber, 1949: 17–19, 22–6, 50–59, 89–101).

Hayek greatly admired Weber, especially for denying that history exhibits discoverable laws and for advocating methodological individualism in social inquiry. He could not, however, accept Weber's conclusion, with its deep Nietzschean overtones, that ideals lack a foundation, that there is no rational basis for judging one to be superior to another, and that the decision among them is ultimately an arbitrary one, based on an act of faith or sheer will – like choosing between God and the Devil. To be sure, the political philosopher, by Hayek's reckoning, must not be 'afraid of deciding between conflicting values.' He recognises 'that he must choose which he should accept and which reject' (114–15). Nevertheless, Hayek looks for some foundation for this choice and refuses to see it as only a matter of faith or subjective will.

Hayek's alternative is to put forward his ideal, the Rule of Law, as a meta-legal principle. He does not tell us much about the status of this principle, but clearly it must be understood in light of his foundational teachings in Part I. Hayek has emphasised that 'we can never synthetically construct a new body of moral rules' (63). We must accept much of 'the undirected and spontaneously grown' (69). Human civilisation 'has a life of its own,' and 'all our efforts to improve things must operate within a working whole which we cannot entirely control.' Hayek's ideal or meta-legal principle must be viewed in these terms: its purpose is not to construct a new body of moral rules, but to identify those rules that have favoured the progress of civilisation; and in this respect it has a foundation or ground.

Progress is favoured chiefly by freedom. Progress cannot be designed, and its direction cannot be anticipated. Our best hope of improving things is to protect individual freedom. The Rule of Law is strictly about freedom. It says nothing about the ends that individuals should pursue or about the long-term consequences of human action.

According to Hayek, the evolutionary process selects out moral rules that favour a society's survival or flourishing. In the second Cairo Lecture, he portrays the ideal of the Rule of Law, as it developed in nineteenth-century Germany, in such terms:

> Like most of the governing ideas of any age, it was held not because its *rationale* was fully understood, but rather because the success of the groups and civilizations who had held it had brought it [the Rule of Law] to dominance. It had become part of that sense of justice which a process of natural selection among societies produces by making those flourish which have evolved beliefs most conductive to the best use of the capacities of their members. (1955: 26)

The point to be underscored is this: with hindsight we

recognise that adherence to the Rule of Law has promoted such social ends as survival, success or flourishing; but since the future is open and uncertain, Hayek seldom justifies his ideal in terms of its likely consequences. The Rule of Law is strictly about freedom. It is constructed from evolved moral rules that safeguard liberty. Its aim is to protect individual freedom here and now and to open up the possibility of human development.

The Rule of Law is an outgrowth of Western civilisation, but Hayek puts it forward as a universal ideal and not one just for Western nations. He provides no clear explanation as to how a particular ideal becomes a standard for all, but he does suggest two possibilities: the Rule of Law offers a pattern for nations that aspire to match the creative achievements of the West; or since modernity has produced a universal civilisation, shaped by Western ideas and institutions, the West's guiding ideal is now the standard for civilisation as such.

Detractors of the Rule of Law

Chapter 16 examines 'The Decline of the Law.' This decline began in Germany soon after institutions designed to secure the Rule of Law were completed. Political and theoretical views emerged that strongly opposed limiting authority by rules of law. They sought 'to give the organized forces of government greater power to shape social relations deliberately according to some ideal of social justice' (235). Opinion soon turned against free institutions, making them incapable of serving their intended aims.

Chapter 16 is mostly about legal theories that rejected or redefined the Rule of Law. They originated in Germany, but soon came to have wide influence in other Western countries, such as

Russia, the UK and the USA. We need only consider what Hayek says about legal positivism.

Legal positivism developed in direct opposition to the natural law tradition. Hayek, of course, has his own objections to natural law theory, but shares its view that a community's laws must be measured by a higher standard – one that is 'found' and not simply created or willed. For legal positivism, 'law by definition consists exclusively of deliberate commands of a human will;' and no higher standard exists by which to measure these commands. The implication is that there can be no limits to the legislator's will. Such rules as the state authority enacts must be accepted as legal, so that the distinction between 'legal' enactments and 'illegal' ones ceases to be valid.

Legal positivism came to be widely accepted after World War I. Its most consistent and influential formulation is to be found in Hans Kelsen's 'pure theory of law.' Kelsen embraced and articulated legal positivism's far-reaching implications: what the legislator wills or commands is law; this will is unlimited; there are no fundamental liberties that the legislator is bound to respect; and a despotic state can have the character of a legal order. By the end of the 1920s, legal positivism had conquered German opinion and was 'spreading rapidly to the rest of the world,' helping to justify the rise of despotism in Hitler's Germany, Fascist Italy and Soviet Russia (238–9; 1955: 22).

From the outset legal positivism opposed 'those meta-legal principles which underlie the ideal of the rule of law' – principles that it dismissed as 'metaphysical superstition.' More fundamentally, it redefined the concept, so that any state 'whose whole activity takes place on the basis of laws and in legal form' is in conformity with the Rule of Law (238). The Rule of Law came to

mean nothing more than 'the demand for legality, the requirement of a legal foundation for any act of the state.' It thereby
'ceased to have any significance as a guarantee of individual
freedom, since any oppression, however arbitrary or discriminatory, could be legalized by a law authorizing an authority to act
in such a manner' (1955: 27). Hayek does detect some signs of a
reaction against legal positivism and similar doctrines (247–9),
but there remains an urgent need to clarify and restore the Rule
of Law.

7 ORIGINS AND DEVELOPMENT OF THE RULE OF LAW (CHAPTERS 11, 12, 13)

Hayek devotes three chapters to the origins of the Rule of Law and to its institutional and conceptual development. These chapters focus in turn on England during the seventeenth and eighteenth centuries, on America during its founding period, and on Germany between 1800 and the 1870s. Hayek's emphasis throughout is on the growth of institutions that embody aspects of the Rule of Law and on ideas that convey its basic principles. This fits with his intention to show that the Rule of Law, as an ideal, is not simply a rational construction, but the result of an evolutionary process, where emerging beliefs and unintended consequences made possible an articulation of the principles of individual freedom. The contributions of England, America and Germany are presented as parts of a single process of growth or as 'stages in a continuous development' (202). Each nation added something distinctive during its shining moment. There is no chapter on France, since Hayek judges that political and intellectual developments there, after the Revolution, were largely unfavourable to his ideal (194–6).

English origins

When and where did individual freedom originate? Contrary to some interpretations, Hayek insists that such freedom was known to the ancients, particularly in Athens at the time of its greatness and in late republican Rome. In fact, what classical authors said about individual freedom and its legal protections would greatly influence modern thought (164–7). Hayek's interest, however, is not in the ancient world, but in the modern origins of individual freedom, understood both as the general condition of a people and as an ideal.

The modern evolution of the Rule of Law began in seventeenth-century England. This evolution, as traced by Hayek, involves both events and ideas, with events and their unforeseen consequences taking priority. Thus he observes that English liberty 'appeared first, as it probably always does, as a by-product of a struggle for power rather than as the result of deliberate aim' (162). Hayek refers here to the great struggle between king and Parliament that began soon after Elizabeth's death in 1603 and convulsed seventeenth-century England; the liberty of the individual 'emerged [from it] as a by-product' (167). The conflict with Parliament was provoked by the economic policies of Elizabeth's successors, particularly their attempts to establish industrial monopolies and to impose severe regulations on economic activity. These policies led to demands for 'equal laws for all citizens' and for adherence to 'the certain rule of law,' as distinguished from uncertain and arbitrary government. Ways to limit royal discretion and bring the king under the law were discussed extensively and continuously throughout the Civil War. From this discussion there gradually emerged all the political ideals 'which were thenceforth to govern English political evolution' (168).

The evolutionary process that Hayek is describing was highly compressed. By 1660, when the Stuart monarchy was restored, the ideas of liberty advanced in preceding decades 'had become part of an established tradition.' Hayek's account of seventeenth-century England details a massive and rapid shift in opinion regarding the kind of government that could legitimately claim the people's obedience. This is significant, because 'power is ultimately not a physical fact but a state of opinion which makes people obey' (181). Hayek further observes that 'a group of men can form a society capable of making laws because they already share common beliefs which make discussion and persuasion possible and to which the articulated rules must conform in order to be accepted as legitimate' (181). The prevalence of such common beliefs explains how Parliament, in the Glorious Revolution of 1688, could with little bloodshed depose the ruling monarch and install a new one. The emergent ideas of liberty subsequently became part of the doctrine of the victorious Whig party. John Locke's major achievement was to codify Whig doctrine, thereby setting forth the practical principles that should, by common agreement, thereafter control government's powers (169–71). While Hayek is largely critical of Locke's speculations on the foundations of government, he applauds his 'codification' of the accepted political doctrine.

The first half of the eighteenth century was the main period of consolidation, during which time the ideal of the Rule of Law 'progressively penetrated everyday practice.' Most of the principles for which Englishmen of the previous century had fought were slowly but steadily extended. Indeed, 'the principles themselves ceased to be a matter of [partisan] dispute;' and the Tories came fully to accept them (171–2). Later in the century, 'coherent expositions' of English ideals were put forward, chiefly by Hume, Burke and William Paley. Other leading writers, including Adam

Smith and William Blackstone, took these ideals for granted, but largely refrained from stating them explicitly (172–4).

England's major contribution to the evolution of the principles of freedom ended with the close of the eighteenth century. Its achievements were mostly preserved beyond the nineteenth century, but there was little further development of underlying ideals, even in the writings of historians such as T. B. Macaulay and of economists in the Smithian tradition. There emerged a new, constructivist liberalism, often guided by the ideals of the French Revolution, which scorned Britain's received constitution and proposed 'to remake the whole of her law and institutions on rational principles.' Here Hayek mentions Bentham and the Utilitarians as well as the moralist and radical pamphleteer Richard Price. From this point forward the English ideal of individual liberty was progressively displaced, even in Great Britain, by 'the essentially French concept of political liberty' (174–5).

America's contribution

The colonists who settled America brought with them the principles of individual freedom that had developed in England, including 'the conception that no power should be arbitrary and that all power should be limited by higher law' (177). What Americans added was an insistence on a fixed constitution, a written document that recognises fundamental principles and organises government around them. This conviction – that the protection of freedom requires a written constitution – was rooted in America's early experience with compacts and charters. It found expression in the various state constitutions that were established during and after the Revolution, and it stimulated efforts to draft a constitution for the USA. Hayek calls this belief and practice 'constitutionalism;' and he regards constitutionalism as America's distinctive contribution to the growth of the Rule of Law.

American constitutionalism presents something of a challenge to Hayek's outlook. The federal Constitution, like the various state constitutions that were formed after the Revolution, arose from an effort deliberately to construct a basic framework of laws and also to achieve something unprecedented in the annals of government. In this respect it can be viewed as both constructivist and anti-traditional. Hayek acknowledges that the American founders were, in a sense, 'guided by a spirit of rationalism, a desire for deliberate construction and pragmatic procedure closer to what we have called the "French tradition" than to the "British."' Furthermore, they exhibited 'a general suspicion of tradition and an exuberant pride in the fact that the new structure was entirely of their own making.'

Hayek insists, however, that the American founders were 'essentially mistaken' as to what they were achieving. The governmental framework that ultimately emerged from the federal Constitution was different 'from any clearly foreseen structure,' and 'much of the outcome was due to historical accident or the application of inherited principles to a new situation.' The vaunted 'new discoveries' of the Constitution either 'resulted from the application of traditional principles to particular problems' or else 'emerged as only dimly perceived consequences of general ideas' (183–4).

American constitutionalism, besides requiring a fixed and written document, incorporated numerous ways of limiting government and making it conform to general rules. In this connection Hayek discusses the appeal to higher law, the division of powers both among the branches of the federal government and between government and the states, the insistence on the inviolable rights of individuals, and the practice of judicial review. A thread running through the entire discussion is the problem of how, in popular government, majorities can be kept within safe limits.

The Americans were much more concerned than the English had been with limiting the power of representative legislatures. Partly this was because the colonists, in the decade leading up to the Revolution, had been forced to resist Parliament's claim to power over them; but more fundamentally it reflected awareness that, in a democratic society, majority rule could endanger liberty. The newly formed state legislatures were frequently criticised at the time for exceeding their proper powers.

Americans embraced the long-standing view that ordinary legislation must conform to a 'higher law;' and they insisted on codifying higher law principles in a written document, so as to make them explicit and enforceable. This means that particular laws enacted by the legislature are just only if they conform to principles embodied in the Constitution. Requiring conformity to general principles deters the legislature from sacrificing long-term advantages to immediate aims and from conferring privileges or imposing penalties on individuals (179–80).

Hayek's view of higher law differs substantially from the way the Americans themselves understood it. By his interpretation, higher law is not rooted in divine will, or nature, or reason, as Americans had generally believed. Hayek reminds us that reason always 'moves within a non-rational framework of beliefs and institutions.' Higher law, for any society, consists of principles implicit in prevailing beliefs and opinions. The decisive consideration is whether a people, regardless of how they understand the source of higher principles, resolves to follow them long-term. By doing so, a people gains 'more control over the general nature of the political order than they would possess if its character were to be determined solely by successive decisions of a particular character' (181–2).

American constitutionalism was centrally concerned with limiting representative legislatures. To this end, the federal Constitution divided power among three branches of government, enumerated legislative powers, and opened the door for the judiciary to invalidate laws that conflict with the Constitution. Hayek is silent about some crucial checks on the US Congress – its division into two 'Houses' which must agree with each other to enact laws, and the presidential veto.

As for the executive, Hayek is critical of constitutional provisions that 'led to the formation of a presidential republic.' Under this arrangement, 'the chief executive derives his power directly from the people and, in consequence, may belong to a different party from that which controls the legislature.' Hayek objects that this arrangement erects an 'obstacle to the efficiency of the executive;' but later he suggests a deeper reason for avoiding a presidential republic – the prospect that the executive, in the name of the people, will undertake measures that endanger freedom. Thus Franklin D. Roosevelt, convinced that he knew best how to deal with the Great Depression, 'conceived it as the function of democracy in times of crisis to give unlimited powers to the man it trusted.' Among other measures, Roosevelt attempted in 1937 to gain control of the Supreme Court by increasing its size and packing it with judges who supported his policies. This effort was defeated in the US Senate – a case where the legislature acted to curb unwarranted executive power (186, 190–91).

The issue of majority rule is central to Hayek's discussion of American constitutionalism. Mainly he relies on a distinction that the American founders had employed, one between the majority's often ill-considered short-term will and its more deliberate long-term will. The Constitution's democratically minded critics fault it for structuring government so as to thwart the majority will. Hayek replies that 'a constitutional system does not involve an absolute limitation of the will of the people but merely a subordination of immediate objectives to long-term ones.' Thus the people agree 'to submit to the will of the temporary majority on particular issues' on 'the understanding that this majority will abide by more general principles laid down beforehand by a more comprehensive body,' such as a constitutional convention (179–80).

Culmination in Germany

Each of the nations that contributed to the growth of the Rule of Law responded to a particular threat to individual freedom: England to arbitrary monarchical power; America to representative legislatures and majorities fixed on short-term goals; and Germany to the administrative state.

The 'German people' had a complex political history during the period of Hayek's review, and it is sometimes difficult to tell just which phase of that history or which German states he has in mind. The German Confederation was formed in 1815, following the defeats of Napoleon. It was comprised of 39 states, with Prussia and Austria being the dominant members. In 1866, with the victory of Prussia and its German allies in the Austro-Prussian War, the German Confederation was dissolved; and that year the North German Confederation was established by Prussia and north German states. Prussia's growing dominance and its 1870 victory in the Franco-Prussian War led to the formation in 1871 of the German Empire as a constitutional monarchy, with King Wilhelm of Prussia as German Emperor and Otto von Bismarck as Chancellor.

Hayek gives a mixed verdict on Prussian influence. Looking back to the eighteenth century, he credits Frederick II's civil code of 1751 with initiating a rapidly spreading movement 'for the codification of all the laws.' Hayek regards this movement 'as one of the most important aspects of the endeavor on the Continent to establish the rule of law' (197). In this atmosphere Immanuel Kant and later the young Wilhelm von Humboldt wrote highly influential treatises on moral and educational freedom; and liberal movements emerged with the broad aim of limiting government by a constitution and general laws. Yet by the 1860s and 1870s, Prussia had become a 'police state,' defeating efforts to bring Prussia itself and the broader political entities it dominated under the Rule of Law (199–200).

The liberal movement in Germany had two main goals: establishing the *Rechtsstaat* (or law state) and achieving the ideal of constitutionalism. In the Cairo Lectures, Hayek gives considerable attention to writers, especially in southern Germany, who helped develop the theoretical conception of the *Rechtsstaat* after 1800; but he omits this review in Chapter 13 of *The Constitution of Liberty* (cf. 1955: 21–3).

The *Rechtsstaat* was designed primarily to curb the arbitrary exercise of power by the expanding bureaucracy. In all of continental Europe, and especially in Prussia, there developed 'a powerful centralized administrative machinery' with 'a body of professional administrators who had become the main rulers of the people' (193). Initially liberals saw their choice as one between either depending on the ordinary courts to decide whether administrative acts were lawful and consistent with private rights or, in line with French practice, establishing 'quasi-judicial bodies inside the administrative machinery' to decide on the lawfulness of administrative acts (196, 199–201). For a long time the liberal supporters of the *Rechtsstaat* advocated the first approach, which would depend on the ordinary courts to limit the administration. This approach came to be known as 'justicialism.' By the 1860s liberals had turned to a different conception, which in effect modified the first approach so as to avoid placing judicial responsibility inside the administration.

Rudolf von Gneist was the main architect of the new system. Von Gneist and his supporters called for the creation of a separate system of courts, alongside the regular ones, to hear cases involving administrative actions. These 'were meant to be completely independent courts,' not judicial bodies inside the administrative apparatus; and it was hoped that they would, in the course of time, 'assume a strictly judicial control over all administrative action.' To defend these special courts, advocates reasoned that 'the ordinary judge, trained mainly in private or criminal law,' cannot be expected to possess the specialised knowledge required to settle disputes over administrative actions. This argument won over liberal supporters of the Rule of Law. Thereafter the *Rechtsstaat* came to mean a system of independent administrative courts rather than a reliance on the ordinary courts. Indeed, this new approach was seen as the *Rechtsstaat*'s crowning achievement. Most German administrative lawyers backed it; and a system along these lines was introduced in the German states in the 1860s and 1870s (200–202).

Liberal hopes of imposing independent judicial control over an entrenched bureaucracy would be disappointed: 'Just as the new device was introduced, there commenced a major reversal of intellectual trends' – a reversal that was occasioned by the 'new movement toward state socialism and the welfare state.' This new movement began to gather force in the 1870s and 1880s, just as the system of administrative courts received its final shape in the German states. The new movement favoured widening administrative discretion rather than confining it by judicial review. Consequently the liberal conception of the Rule of Law, whose centrepiece had been the *Rechtsstaat*, was abandoned as a practical measure. The Germans were thus 'the last people that the liberal tide reached before it began to recede' (202).

Hayek warns us not to underrate the theoretical achievement of German liberals. Despite their lack of political success, they were the ones who applied the old ideal of the Rule of Law to the problem of restraining the modern administrative state: 'they represent in some respects the last stage in a continuous development and are perhaps better adapted to the problems of our time than many of the older institutions.' The rise of the administrative state began in continental Europe; but in the twentieth century, it ascended in Britain and the USA as well. Thus the 'power of the professional administrator ... is now the main threat to individual liberty;' and the 'institutions developed in Germany for the purpose of keeping him in check deserve more careful examination than they have been given' (202).

In this context Hayek criticises A. V. Dicey, whose study of the English constitution he generally praises, for making 'the possibility of a review of administrative acts by the *ordinary* courts' the chief test of the Rule of Law. Dicey here overlooked the independent administrative courts that were central to the idea and practice of the *Rechtsstaat*. In this way Dicey contributed much 'to prevent or delay the growth of institutions which could subject the new bureaucratic machinery to effective control.' His influence 'blocked the development which would have offered the best chance of preserving' the Rule of Law (203–4).

8 REQUIREMENTS OF THE RULE OF LAW (CHAPTER 14)

The Rule of Law defines the attributes of 'true law' and also identifies the institutions that are required to safeguard individual liberty. Hayek enumerates these attributes and safeguards in both the Cairo Lectures and *The Constitution of Liberty* (Chapter 14), but with some important variations. This enumeration is not presented as a rational system, but rather as 'a complex of doctrines which have been formulated at different times and which are connected only by serving the same end' (1955: 34). This view fits Hayek's claim that his 'ideal' is a product of undirected growth rather than logical construction.

True law promotes freedom by safeguarding the private sphere

The end served by the Rule of Law, broadly stated, is to promote liberty by making individuals secure against governmental encroachments on the private sphere. More specifically, it 'is to limit coercion by the power of the state to instances where it is explicitly required by general abstract rules which have been announced beforehand and which [are] applied equally to all people, and refer to circumstances known to them' (ibid.: 34; cf. 1960: 208). Government coerces individuals chiefly by punishing them. Under the Rule of Law, it can 'infringe a person's protected private sphere only as punishment for breaking an announced general rule' (206). Here and elsewhere, Hayek distinguishes sharply between general laws that the ordinary citizen must observe and those acts of legislative authority, which amount to orders, that instruct servants of the state 'concerning the manner in which they are to direct the apparatus of government and the means which are at their disposal' (207). Government has broad discretion to command how its particular resources will be used, but it cannot order about the private individual as if he were a mere governmental resource.

True law is known and certain

The laws must be made known or promulgated, since they shape the environment in which we plan our actions. If individuals know what rules they can count on, they are better able to predict the outcome of their actions, determine their responsibilities, and use their knowledge effectively. Known and certain laws are vital to economic life; and they promote the spontaneous growth of social order. They enable people to 'foresee with a high degree of confidence what collaboration they can expect from others,' thus facilitating the 'mutual adjustment of individuals' that produces order spontaneously. Hayek emphasises that the law's relative certainty makes court decisions predictable, thus reducing litigation and enabling a free society to run more smoothly and efficiently. These considerations lead him to conclude that 'the task of the lawgiver is not to set up a particular order but merely to create conditions in which an orderly arrangement can establish and ever renew itself' (208–9; cf. 159–61).

True law is both general and equal

Generality or abstractness is a necessary feature of law. Hayek had made this clear particularly by distinguishing in Chapter 10 between laws and commands. A command is an order to someone to take a particular action or refrain from it; and it presupposes someone who has issued the command. A law, by contrast, 'is directed to unknown people,' and it speaks in an impersonal voice. It abstracts 'from all particular circumstances of time and place' and 'refers only to such conditions as may occur anywhere and at any time.' Hayek grants that these distinctions are not hard and fast, since laws 'shade gradually into commands as their content becomes more specific' (149–50).

The principle of generality does not, however, encompass the requirement that 'any law should apply equally to all.' A law might be general and yet make different provisions for different classes of persons and, where classes are defined narrowly, implicitly favour specific individuals. Complete equality before the law means 'that no attribute belonging to some individuals but not to others should alter their position under the law' (1955: 36). Hayek insists that we should strive towards this goal, but grants that it 'is probably both unattainable and undesirable' (ibid.: 36). He does not object in principle to laws that single out a particular group, e.g. women, or the blind, or people above a certain age, so long as the legitimacy of the distinction is acknowledged by those inside the group as well as those outside it. Yet ideally, equality of the law aims to equally improve 'the chances of yet unknown persons' and is 'incompatible with benefiting or harming known persons in a predictable manner' (209–10, 153–5).

Hayek denies that justice is an attribute of law, independent of its generality, certainty and equality. If a law 'confines itself to regulating the relations between different persons and does not interfere with the purely private concerns of an individual,' we have no test for its compatibility with a reign of freedom 'other than its generality and equality' (210). Here, as in Chapter 6, Hayek interprets the principle of equality to mean that the law should treat people alike in spite of inequalities that arise from nature and from nurture. Equality before the law increases the de facto inequalities among individuals, but these are advantageous to a free society. Also, the Rule of Law is at odds with the quest for distributive justice. Those who pursue it 'will in practice find themselves obstructed at every move by the rule of law.' Distributive justice requires government to decide what different individuals will receive or reward them according to someone's conception of their merit. The Rule of Law demands, however, that individuals be treated equally under general laws, without regard to their particular qualities or circumstances (232).

The laws consist of 'general rules that apply equally to everybody.' It follows that those persons who enact and apply the laws must also be subject to them. This requirement – that the laws apply equally to those who govern as well as to any private person – reduces the risk that the state and its agents will act oppressively (210).

The Rule of Law requires an independent judiciary

Hayek hesitates to make the 'separation of powers' a blanket requirement of the Rule of Law, since this doctrine has a variety of meanings, some of which Hayek disapproves of. He does insist, however, that the judiciary should constitute 'a separate power' from the legislature. The Rule of Law means that 'the laying-down of new general rules' must be separate from 'their application to particular cases.' These two functions 'must be performed separately by two co-ordinated bodies before it can be determined whether coercion is to be used in a particular case.' In practice, this requires 'independent judges who are not concerned with any temporary ends of government' (210–11). These judges 'are bound by nothing but the law and secured against all pressure by irremovability and similar safeguards' (1955: 37). This arrangement helps to ensure that rules are made because of their general significance and not to fit particular instances.

Judicial decision-making, as Hayek understands it, looks beyond particular statutes and their intent. In fact, the judge has no concern with 'the hidden intentions of the maker of the rules' (ibid.: 37). The judge's task is 'to discover the implications contained in the spirit of the whole system of valid rules of law.' When necessary, he expresses as a general rule 'what was not explicitly stated previously in a court of law or by the legislator' (212). Clearly a great deal of discernment is required to grasp the spirit of the laws, to determine its implications for the case at hand, and to express this as a general rule. The judge makes explicit much that the law itself leaves unstated; and inevitably 'certain general conceptions' will enter into the judge's interpretation of the law. Even so, Hayek measures judicial interpretation by an objective standard, namely 'what the rules as they have been promulgated must mean to an impartial observer' (1955: 37).

The separation-of-powers doctrine, in some formulations, prohibits the general legislature from delegating the rule-making function to other bodies; but Hayek rejects this limitation. From the standpoint of the Rule of Law, he sees nothing wrong with delegating the power of making rules 'to local legislative bodies, such as provincial assemblies or municipal councils' or even in some instances to 'some non-elective authority,' so long as this authority announces these rules prior to their application and is made to adhere to them. What Hayek objects to in modern practice is not delegating legislation, but giving authorities 'power to wield coercion without rule' and expecting the courts to accept the exercise of such power unquestioningly (1960: 211–12; 1955: 38–9).

The executive, in coercing private citizens, is subject to legislative rules and to judicial review

The primary function of the government or executive is to protect the individual against coercion by others and thus to safeguard for each individual a secure private sphere. To this end the executive enjoys a monopoly of coercive power. This function is to be distinguished from the executive's administrative or policy function, which is not inherently coercive, but may become so under a regime of central planning. Hayek insists that with the rise of the modern bureaucratic state, individual liberty is now mainly threatened by administrative power (see 202). Thus it is hardly surprising that *The Constitution of Liberty* devotes far more attention to administration than to lawmaking or judging.

Deciding where the executive stands, in relation to the legislature and to the courts, is, for Hayek, a major problem that is addressed throughout Parts II and III, especially when matters of 'discretion' and 'policy' are discussed. Hayek regards the legislature and the courts as distinct and separate powers, but he denies that this is the case with the executive. The decisive consideration here is not the executive's monopoly of coercion, which arguably makes it more powerful than the legislature and the courts, but its dependence on the other powers. The legislature and the judiciary are independent of each other in that one formulates rules and the other interprets them. The executive, however, is bound in its coercive actions 'by rules which prescribe not only when and where it may use coercion but also in what manner it may do so.' Moreover, all of its actions of this kind are subject to judicial review. Hayek's aim here is to hem in the executive, insofar as its use of coercion is concerned, by subordinating it to legislative rules, on the one hand, and judicial review, on the other. In this respect it is not 'independent' and therefore not a separate power (211).

Hayek grants that administrators, like judges, must interpret legislative rules in order to apply them, but the substance of their interpretation must be subject to review by an independent court. In such a review, the court will impose a very strict test, deciding whether the administrative decision is 'deducible from the rules of law and from those circumstances to which the law refers and which can be known to the private parties affected' (1955: 41; 1960: 213–14). When it comes to protecting the individual from coercion and securing impartial justice, independent courts must have the last word.

The Rule of Law safeguards fundamental rights and civil liberties

Hayek's case for freedom is not built around the idea of individual rights, but, nonetheless, rights are vital to his account of the Rule of Law. These are not to be understood as natural rights, in the Lockean sense, but as rights that have evolved historically and have found expression in various constitutional provisions. What can statements of rights add to the general argument for freedom? After all, under 'a reign of freedom the free sphere of the individual includes all action not explicitly restricted by a general law' (216). If the individual enjoys the freedom (or right) to do whatever a general law does not restrict, then what is gained by enumerating specific rights? And since any enumeration is necessarily incomplete, isn't there a danger of depreciating rights that aren't explicitly recognised? Hayek acknowledges this danger, but concludes that bills of rights have in the past afforded 'an important protection for certain rights known to be easily endangered' (216).

In the Cairo Lectures, Hayek identifies the rights associated with 'life, liberty, and property,' along with liberty of speech, religion, the press and assembly, as essential ones; and he stresses the right to private property in particular, since rules of property determine 'the boundaries of individual private spheres in the material world, and ways of voluntarily changing these boundaries' (1955: 44). Hayek's emphasis in *The Constitution of Liberty* is on how rights are endangered by advancing technologies (216). He acknowledges the importance of procedural safeguards, but does not expect that they will remain effective if belief in the Rule of Law is weakened (218–19).

How do bills of rights serve to protect individual freedom? Hayek grants that neither legal guarantees of fundamental rights nor constitutional provisions can, in themselves, 'prevent any suppression of rights by the deliberate action of the ultimate legislator' (217). We recall that the ultimate legislator, in democracies, is the people, or, more precisely, public opinion or the prevailing sense of justice (1955: 33; 1960: 217). Constitutional formulations of individual rights serve to 'impress upon the public mind' the value of these rights. They become 'part of a political creed which the people will defend even when they do not fully understand its significance' (217).

Emergency powers, just compensation and the public interest

After listing the attributes of true law, Hayek discusses government's emergency powers. Here he addresses, in a somewhat indirect way, the vital question of how and when the Rule of Law is to be applied. Hayek assumes that applications of the Rule of Law must be governed by the public interest. This implies that protection for individual rights can be suspended where the interest of the community requires it.

In *The Constitution of Liberty*, Hayek argues as follows: legal guarantees of individual freedom are basic to 'the normal running of society,' but they are not 'absolute rights' that can never be infringed: 'Even the most fundamental principles of a free society ... may have to be temporarily sacrificed when, but only when, it is a question of preserving liberty in the long run.' Such a sacrifice of individual liberties might be necessary in a time of war, requiring a suspension of habeas corpus protections and even the imposition of 'a state of siege.'

Having made these points, Hayek turns quickly from broad emergency powers to narrower ways in which government, acting in 'the public interest,' might justifiably infringe particular liberties. Two such cases, which 'can hardly be disputed,' are curtailing freedom of speech in a situation of 'clear and present danger' and compulsory land purchase through government's right of eminent domain.[1] Hayek goes on to insist that such cases should conform to a rule, so that they can be reviewed by an independent court, and that individuals who are affected should receive full compensation, both as a matter of justice and as a deterrent to government arbitrariness (217–18).

Hayek's third Cairo Lecture makes roughly the same points, but with this important difference: it offers a much more detailed rationale for emergency powers. As Hayek reminds us, the Rule of Law establishes a sphere 'in which the individual can follow his own will' and also know clearly 'the conditions and the manner in which he can be coerced.' Nevertheless, the individual's private sphere is not sacrosanct under all conditions. Exceptional circumstances will arise 'in which it would be in the highest interest of the Community that particular individuals should be made to do things as a result of events which they do not know and in a manner for which no rule provides.' These exceptional circumstances include 'natural catastrophes' and 'war or other sudden dangers.' Such events call for swift and concerted action, so that even the private citizen may be required to 'place himself under the command of authority.'

Emergency powers must be exercised by 'guardians of the public interest.' These guardians must be kept in check, however, by an independent court, which will 'decide on general abstract principles not only about the legitimacy of the interference but also about the appropriate compensation.' The community, which benefited from the exercise of emergency powers, must bear the cost of compensating the individual fully for every infringement of his right of private property or of 'other legally acquired rights' (1955: 44–5).

---

1   'Eminent domain' is the phrase often used in the USA to describe what is generally known simply as 'compulsory purchase' in the UK.

Hayek does not here identify the well-informed 'guardians of the common interest' who will exercise emergency powers. One might assume that he has in mind the executive, or some portion of it, or perhaps the judges who review the executive's actions. When Hayek returns to this topic much later, he assigns these powers to 'an emergency committee of the Legislative Assembly,' which would be 'entitled to grant limited emergency powers until the Assembly as a whole could be convened.' The full Assembly would then 'determine both the extent and duration of the emergency powers granted to government' (1979: 125).

Hayek seems to count on the executive's acquiescence to the courts and to the legislature when its use of emergency powers is called into question. Accordingly he is silent here about the possible need to curb an obdurate or despotic government. Liberalism in its classical or Lockean form had assigned this responsibility ultimately to the community or to the people. It taught that the community, which is the source of political power, may resist and depose a government that consistently abuses its power (see *Second Treatise*, nos 222–30 and 240–43). The American Declaration of Independence puts it this way: if government persists in violating the ends for which it was formed, then 'it is the right of the people to alter or to abolish it' and to institute new government of such principles and form as shall seem to them 'most likely to effect their safety and happiness.'

This is not Hayek's kind of liberalism. He grants that community opinion is the ultimate authority in policy matters, but gives no hint that the community might forcibly change an abusive government. Generally speaking, Hayek opposes violent ruptures with the past: 'Perhaps no violent revolution is likely to increase the respect for the law' (194). He is critical in particular of the

French Revolution, as it eventually unfolded, and of the line of modern political thought that it inspired. At the same time he applauds conservative writers who not only opposed the French Revolution, but identified progress with undirected growth and respect for tradition (see 55–6, 174–5, 194–5 and 400).

To summarise, the Rule of Law aims to secure individual freedom, partly by identifying rights that government must protect. This ideal is constant, but its application depends on what best serves the community's interest under prevailing conditions. Suspending individual rights is justified if the community's safety is at stake. When it comes to the use of emergency powers, Hayek reasons that a short-term sacrifice of liberty may be required for its long-term preservation. There remains, however, the question of what limits on freedom are permissible in 'normal' times, as measured by the public interest. In the absence of an emergency, can government, acting for the community's benefit, justifiably curb the liberty of individuals and coerce them, even if they have not disobeyed the law or violated anyone's private sphere? Hayek opens this door by referring to government's right of compulsory purchase. Are there other, more essential examples? We will find an answer to this question shortly.

9 ECONOMIC POLICY AND THE RULE OF LAW (CHAPTER 15)

Hayek is primarily concerned in Chapter 15 with the problem of shaping and limiting government's economic policies. Most of his examples show how economic life is affected, for better or worse, by administrative measures. Hayek thus needs criteria by which to measure and judge economic policies; but to articulate them, he must look broadly at government's policy role and consider what government may and may not do, under the Rule of Law, in executing its policies. His observations about economics are framed by these more general reflections on policy. In discussing these matters, Hayek presupposes or restates much of what he has said earlier about law and coercion and about the relation of the executive or administration to the lawmaking body. This chapter is vital for the rest of his book, since it lays the foundation for Hayek's extended treatment, in Part III, of specific policy areas.

What is policy?

Hayek's most illuminating definition of policy appears in Chapter 14, in a brief section entitled 'Legislation and Policy.' He begins by dispelling the idea that legislation itself is a policy matter, or that the law is the chief instrument for carrying out some predetermined long-term policy. The work of legislation is to establish general rules of conduct, within which government must act to achieve its ends. Legislation must not itself specify those ends. Policy, by contrast, 'means the pursuit by government of the concrete, ever changing aims of the day.' Executing policy in this sense is largely the work of administration: 'Its task is the direction and allocation of resources put at the disposal of government in the service of the constantly changing needs of the community' (214–15; cf. Hayek, 1955: 42–3).

These statements bring out two key points about policy. First, government's broad objective in policy matters is to serve the community's needs. Hayek mentions particular services that governments provide to citizens, ranging 'from national defense to upkeep of roads, from sanitary safeguards to the policing of the streets,' but all such policies must serve the needs or interests of the community. Second, government has 'resources' at its disposal, to be used in pursuing its policies. Faced with urgent tasks, it must direct and allocate these resources, which include both its material means and its paid servants. Since professional administrators inevitably grasp for more, Hayek stresses that agencies entrusted with special tasks 'must confine themselves to the means specially granted to them' (215). A crucial question, left unanswered at this point, is how government obtains its material resources.

Tests of policy

The Rule of Law governs all government's policy actions, but does not necessarily limit or restrict them. The essential question is whether a specific policy involves coercion: 'It is ... important to remember that the rule of law restricts government only in its coercive activities' (206; cf. 1955: 22). If a government policy is coercive, it must conform to the principles of the Rule of Law. Hayek distinguishes between coercive measures and 'those pure service activities where coercion does not enter or does so only because of the need of financing them by taxation' (222). The taxation issue aside, these 'pure service activities' would not be restricted by the Rule of Law, unless they were to become coercive.

Assuming that a specific policy is compatible with the Rule of Law, it must then be judged according to its expediency or efficiency. The question here is whether the policy will succeed or fail and whether its advantages will outweigh its costs (221).

Hayek introduces the expediency test to judge how administrative discretion is used. In order to pursue policy objectives in concrete situations, amid ever-changing circumstances, administrators must act according to their judgement of what is best: 'Nobody disputes the fact that, in order to make efficient use of the means at its disposal, the government must exercise a great deal of discretion' (213). Expediency is a test of whether discretionary actions are efficient in reaching their objectives; and economic analysis, especially the weighing of costs and benefits, is crucial in making such judgements. Having discretion allows administrators to choose from a range of legitimate options in deciding on the best course of action. A policy measure can be inexpedient but still in conformity with the Rule of Law. Moreover, an expedient action that harms many is permissible, if the outcome is beneficial overall (224–5).

The ultimate objective of policy – that it must serve the needs or interests of the community – is vital for determining both a policy's compatibility with the Rule of Law and its expediency, as we shall see.

Excluded policies

Some policies are excluded in principle from a free society because they cannot possibly be reconciled with the Rule of Law. These are ones that 'cannot be achieved by merely enforcing general rules but, of necessity, involve arbitrary discrimination between persons' (227; cf. 231). Hayek considers three types of excluded policies, the first of which is giving specific individuals the right to engage in different occupations or to provide services or commodities. Forbidding favouritism of this kind does not, in Hayek's view, preclude setting job qualifications or requiring a licence to practise certain trades, so long as these measures follow a general rule that applies to any qualified person and gives each one the right, if passed over, to 'have his claim examined and enforced by an independent court' (227).

Price controls, whether imposed directly by authority or indirectly by specifying the quantities that particular persons or firms can buy or sell, are incompatible with a free system for two reasons. First, such controls have to be administered arbitrarily and not according to a rule. More broadly, free markets will work only if individual decisions are guided by price movements. In the absence of prices, governments will try unsuccessfully to achieve similar results by direct orders (227–9).

Finally, a government bound by the Rule of Law cannot undertake to reward people according to their supposed merit. Hayek repeats here his oft-stated objection to government pursuing distributive justice: it requires 'an allocation of all resources by a central authority' and also 'that people be told what to do and what ends to serve.' The administrative pursuit of distributive justice is incompatible with treating individuals according to general rules (231–3).

Policies measured by expediency

For policies that are compatible with the Rule of Law and the requirements of a free society, the question is whether their benefits are worth their cost. A wide range of activities, universally undertaken by governments, fall into this category. Some of these furnish information that individuals need to plan their lives. Government's most important function here is providing 'a reliable and efficient monetary system,' but scarcely less important 'are the setting of standards of weights and measures; the providing of information gathered from surveying, land registration, statistics, etc; and the support, if not also the organization, of some kind of education.' Other policies aim to provide more material services. These include sanitary and health services, road construction and maintenance, urban amenities, and 'public works' generally (223).

Hayek does not favour passive government, but rather one that seeks many benefits for the community. While he shares the 'strong presumption against government's actively participating in economic efforts,' he nonetheless states that the 'old formulae of laissez faire or non-intervention do not provide us with an adequate criterion for distinguishing between what is and what is not admissible in a free system' (221, 231; cf. 257–8). As he explains, 'it is the character rather than the volume of government activity that is important.' In economic matters, for example, an active government that assists the spontaneous forces of the market is preferable to a less active one that does the wrong things. In this regard he sees himself as following the best of the classical liberals, such as Adam Smith (220–22).

While Hayek does not object to government providing many services, he does insist strongly on two points. First, these services must be available to all. No citizen can be excluded arbitrarily from their enjoyment. Second, government must not forcibly monopolise the provision of these services or enjoy any special advantage in offering them. If possible private suppliers must be allowed to compete with government enterprise, or at least the door must not be shut to them. Both arbitrary exclusion and sheltered monopoly make state coercion impermissible.

The community's interest

The highest standard for judging policy is neither the Rule of Law nor expediency, but the interest of the community. As noted earlier, government can in emergencies suspend individual rights if the community's interest requires it. In 'normal' times, government, acting within the Rule of Law, pursues an expedient course; but expedient actions must aim towards an end, which ultimately is the community's interest.

What policy measures can be justified by expediency, especially when it comes to coercing individuals? Some of Hayek's formulations suggest that governmental coercion must be limited to cases where individuals have violated the law, especially by harming others: 'Under the rule of law, government can infringe a person's protected private sphere only as punishment for breaking an announced general rule' (206). This statement would indicate that only lawbreakers need fear government's coercive hand. As Hayek proceeds, however, it becomes clear that governmental coercion need not be a form of punishment. Government can coerce even law-abiding individuals if the community's interest requires it, so long as it does so in conformity to a general rule and allows for review by independent courts (225).

Taxation and compulsory military service are prime examples of justifiable coercion where no rules have been broken. Hayek grants that government's resources come from taxation and that taxes are coercive (see 144, 222). Taxpayers are coerced, even though they have not violated the law. Coercive taxation is justified by the community's interest in supplying government with needed resources. As for military service, the community must be protected against its enemies, and protection requires a military force. How can government legitimately compel a draftee to submit to a kind of servitude, kill perhaps innocent people, and even face death himself? Coercing draftees, like taxation, is justifiable on the grounds that it serves the interest of the community.

Generally speaking, the law aims to make state coercion both predictable and avoidable. If I can predict what actions will result in my punishment, I can try to avoid those actions. In the absence of law, state coercion is arbitrary; it is neither predictable nor avoidable. Taxation and compulsory military service occupy something of a middle ground between strict adherence to the Rule of Law and arbitrariness. Taxation and compulsory military service are not to be avoided, but to the extent that they follow some rule, they are at least predictable forms of coercion and therefore are not arbitrary. This consideration largely deprives such policies 'of the evil nature of coercion' (143).

There are other policy measures where Hayek appeals to the community's interest in order to justify coercion. He will follow this path, for example, in arguing that government may force individuals to insure themselves against risk:

Once it becomes the recognized duty of the public to provide for the extreme needs of old age, unemployment, sickness, etc., irrespective of whether the individuals

could and ought to have made provision themselves, and
particularly once help is assured to such an extent that
it is apt to reduce individual efforts, it seems an obvious
corollary to compel them to insure (or otherwise provide)
against those common hazards of life.

Hayek goes on to explain that the 'justification in this case is not that people should be coerced to do what is in their individual interest but that, by neglecting to make provision, they would become a charge to the public' (285–6). Also, government has the right to expropriate property at fair market value to provide such amenities as parks and recreation, 'so long as the community approves this' in full awareness of the costs and alternatives (375). Education up to a minimum standard can be made compulsory. The justification, aside from the contribution to democratic governance, is that 'all of us will be exposed to less risks and will receive more benefits from our fellows if they share with us certain basic knowledge and beliefs' (377). Higher education is not compulsory, but the case for subsidising it 'must rest not on the benefit it confers on the recipient but on the resulting advantages for the community at large' (382–3).

PART III
FREEDOM IN THE WELFARE STATE

10 SOCIALISM IN A NEW GUISE: SOCIAL JUSTICE AND THE WELFARE STATE (CHAPTER 17)

Part III of *The Constitution of Liberty* is devoted to policy. Hayek's aim, as he explains in his Introduction, 'will not be to provide a detailed program of policy but rather to state the criteria by which particular measures must be judged if they are to fit into a regime of freedom.' This he will do by applying principles of freedom 'to some of today's critical economic and social issues' (5). Hayek proceeds to develop chapters on 'Labor Unions and Employment,' 'Social Security,' 'Taxation and Redistribution,' 'The Monetary Framework,' 'Housing and Town Planning,' 'Agriculture and Natural Resources,' and 'Education and Research.' These seven chapters on specific areas of policy are introduced by a chapter entitled 'The Decline of Socialism and the Rise of the Welfare State.'

Advent of the welfare state

Hayek begins by calling attention to a great change that has taken place in the post-war period – one that makes it more difficult to identify and combat freedom's opponents. For a century up to the 1940s, efforts at social reform were inspired primarily by socialism. Reformers shared a conviction that society was moving inevitably towards socialism as its necessary and final goal. Their task, as they saw it, was to gain control of the economy by nationalising the means of production, distribution and exchange. Socialism's ascent to power in Britain after the war added to the sense of its inevitability. In 1944 Hayek had published *The Road to Serfdom*, identifying doctrinaire socialism as a pressing danger to liberty.

Looking back, Hayek concludes that the 1940s 'seems to have marked the high tide' of the advance of this 'European' form of socialism. It was discredited by the manifest failure of nationalisation, which turned out to be less productive than private enterprise, favourable to 'a new arbitrary and more inescapable order of rank,' and dangerous to individual liberty. Hayek would thus be 'tilting at windmills' if he were to now direct his argument against it. This does not mean, however, that socialism no longer threatens freedom. Hoping to recover their influence, socialists stopped referring to themselves as such. They abandoned the programme of nationalisation and instead promoted the idea of wealth redistribution, which all along had been their true aim. The new, nameless socialism resembles the old in its advocacy of central planning and economic control, and its guiding ideal – achieving social justice – remains the same. What has changed is its method. The path to social justice will be wealth distribution instead of nationalisation (253–5).

Hayek and the welfare state

One can say that the new socialism aims at 'the welfare state,' but this concept is imprecise; and Hayek must make some distinctions before proceeding to criticise it. In fact, Hayek's rhetorical task is complicated by his own embrace of what some libertarians in particular would regard as welfare state policies. He points out once more, as in Part II, that the Rule of Law limits only the coercive measures of government, leaving 'a wide field' for its non-coercive or pure service activities, which will clearly need to be financed through taxation (257–8).

How then does Hayek's position differ from the socialists' understanding of the welfare state? Hayek explains this difference partly by contrasting two conceptions of security, one of which (the socialist conception) is at odds with individual liberty. Hayek thinks it proper that government should try to reduce risks common to all, help people provide against them, and assure 'a given minimum of sustenance for all;' but it must not attempt to secure to individuals the income that they are thought to deserve in comparison with other persons. Such a conception of security leads inevitably to arbitrary and coercive measures, since it wants to use government's administrative powers to ensure that particular people get the particular things that they supposedly deserve. As the epigraph to Part III, Hayek uses a passage from Tocqueville[1] to illustrate how a society that seeks security through increasing dependence on the state can drift into despotism and end up losing its liberty (258–62, 251).

---

1   'Above this race of men stands an immense and tutelary power, which takes upon itself alone to secure their gratifications and to watch over their fate. That power is absolute, minute, regular, provident, and mild. It would be like the authority of a parent if, like that authority, its object was to prepare men for manhood; but it seeks, on the contrary, to keep them in perpetual childhood: it is well content that the people should rejoice, provided they think of nothing but rejoicing. For their happiness such a government willingly labors, but it chooses to be the sole agent and the only arbiter of that happiness; it provides for their security, foresees and supplies their necessities, facilitates their pleasures, manages their principal concerns, directs their industry, regulates the descent of property, and subdivides their inheritances; what remains, but to spare them all care of thinking and all the trouble of living?' Alexis de Tocqueville, *Democracy in America*, trans. Henry Reeve, edited by Phillips Bradley (New York: Alfred A. Knopf, 1945): v. II, 318.

Hayek's sharpest criticism of the socialistic welfare state centres on its use of wealth redistribution to achieve social justice. There is a deep conflict between 'the ideal of freedom and the desire to "correct" the distribution of incomes so as to make it more "just."' The pursuit of distributive justice cannot follow general rules. It requires that all resources be centrally allocated according to 'the particular aims and knowledge of the planning authority.' Eventually it leads to 'the command economy.' The Rule of Law checks this pursuit at every turn. It serves freedom by precluding 'all those measures which would be necessary to insure that individuals will be rewarded according to another's conception of merit or desert rather than according to the value that their services have for their fellows' (232).

In examining Hayek's critique of welfare state policies, I will focus on the dangers that he chiefly warns against and the specific alternatives that he offers. I begin with what Hayek regards as the most objectionable feature of the welfare state – its use of social security programmes and progressive taxation to redistribute wealth. To secure freedom, the state must avoid coercing citizens unnecessarily and also prevent them from coercing each other. The welfare state fails on both counts. Its social security and taxation policies are inherently coercive, and it fails to prevent labour unions from coercing workers. Moreover, the welfare state's monetary policy is highly inflationary, and its policies on natural resource use, education and scientific research tend to inhibit progress.

11 SOCIAL SECURITY, TAXATION AND THE REDISTRIBUTION OF WEALTH (CHAPTERS 19 AND 20)

Hayek follows up his general critique of the welfare state with chapters on 'Social Security' and 'Taxation and Redistribution.' Both chapters address the issue of wealth redistribution. The first considers alternative ways of designing social security programmes, while the second considers alternative plans of taxation.

Social security

In discussing social security, Hayek considers ways of protecting individuals against risks associated with old age or permanent disability, sickness and unemployment. He lays out his preferred approach to insuring against need and providing for the needy, contrasts it to existing systems of social security, and speculates about the prospects for replacing or changing the current ones.

Hayek insists that the best and cheapest arrangements for social security are ones that evolve gradually through 'the constant re-evaluation of available resources,' as distinguished from unitary systems that are set up according to some advance design. Unitary systems, once established, are hard to change; and like 'all sheltered monopolies' they 'become inefficient in the course of time' (287). Looking back, Hayek finds that suitable provision for social insurance and relief was emerging in the nineteenth century, when the imposition of centralised government systems blocked this path. In England, social services had developed out of the idea that local communities had a duty to provide relief for the poor. With the growth of large cities, special agencies were organised nationally, often by workers themselves, to provide these services and to insure against risk. Hayek acknowledges that industrial society needs arrangements of this sort and that government should assist in their development (286). He is confident that suitable provision for risk and need will continue to emerge, if not thwarted by governmental policies, and that these emergent arrangements, unlike governmental ones, will be consistent with a free society (291–2).

Hayek favours a government-assisted but decentralised plan that encourages – and even compels – individuals to provide for themselves while also making relief available to the needy. It requires that individuals insure themselves against such risks as sickness, permanent disability and perhaps unemployment. Saving for future needs, especially those of old age, obviously fits with personal responsibility; but Hayek says little here about saving, except to point out that governments everywhere are pursuing inflationary policies that rob the thrifty of much that they have put aside for the future (294–5; cf. 328–9).

As a safety net, Hayek would provide public assistance, in an amount consistent with a society's wealth, to persons in great need. He concedes that such a programme involves 'some redistribution of income.' Nevertheless, preventing destitution and providing a minimum level of welfare are now generally accepted as a public duty – one rooted at least partly in the self-interested 'desire of individuals to protect themselves against the consequences of the extreme misery of their fellows' (285–6,

303). The assured minimum level of assistance should be uniform and should be extended only in cases of 'proved need.' Hayek endorses means tests for welfare eligibility, despite their reliance on discretion, and rejects the widespread notion that such tests are degrading (301, 303–4). Defining need is particularly difficult in the area of healthcare, where medical advances have made it 'more and more clear that there is no limit to the amount that might profitably be spent in order to do all that is objectively possible' (298). Here the benefits to the individual of additional treatment must be weighed against the costs, but the individual himself should 'have a say' in this decision 'and be able, by an additional sacrifice, to get more attention' (299).

On the question of helping the unemployed, Hayek is unwilling to extend relief beyond the uniform minimum that is assured to all, except perhaps in a major depression. He opposes such additional relief partly because it distorts the labour market and partly because it subsidises the extravagant wage demands of labour unions. Hayek does welcome genuine insurance against unemployment wherever this is practicable (300–302).

Because public assistance is extended to all, insuring against risk must be compulsory. Hayek reasons that if public relief is available even to needy individuals who neglect to help themselves, some will fail to make provision against emergencies and many may do so inadequately. The obvious solution is 'to compel' individuals 'to insure (or otherwise provide) against' the hazards associated with old age, unemployment, sickness and so on. As noted earlier, Hayek justifies such coercion on the same principle that he had used earlier in justifying taxation and compulsory military service. Although 'the community' may not force a person to act in his own interest, it may nonetheless compel him to do what is in the community's interest, which is preventing harm to its members. Compulsion is justifiable in this case because people who neglect to make provision 'would become a charge to the public' (286).

Hayek's proposals, as summarised above, are embedded in a scathing critique of unitary, government-controlled social security systems, the original of which was the 'social insurance' arrangement that Otto von Bismarck's government enacted in Germany in the 1880s. Although Bismarck did not ban the private relief agencies that then existed, he decreed that the state would henceforth be the sole provider of such social services through a unified organisation to which everyone protected had to belong. The German plan went beyond compulsory insurance to require 'compulsory membership in a unitary organization controlled by the state' (287).

The German model spread because it was presumed to be the most efficient and economical way to provide universal coverage. Hayek grants that this might be true when centralised plans are first introduced, but holds that relying 'on the gradual evolution of suitable institutions' is a better solution in the long run, even if for a time some needs receive inadequate attention. A centralised design for social services shuts off 'the constant re-evaluation of available resources' and leads to long-term inefficiencies (287; cf. 232).

Hayek goes on to argue that compulsory social service monopolies were mainly attractive to socialists not because of their presumed efficiency, but because they provided a means of egalitarian redistribution. The socialists recognised that a monopolistic government service could distribute benefits according to perceived need and also redistribute income from one group to another, as might seem desirable. These compulsory monopolies were represented to the public as 'social insurance,' but this claim was deceptive.

Insurance, properly speaking, grants protection only to those who can claim it through their contributions. Monopolistic social security programmes, by contrast, enrol those who have not yet had time to establish a claim. People receive 'as a matter of right what they have only to a small extent paid for.' Benefits are not limited to a contractual amount, or even to some necessary minimum, but reflect a political judgement as to an amount that would be adequate, regardless of a person's need or contribution. Unlike genuine insurance, government plans can transfer income from one group to another. Pension claims, for example, are paid out of the taxes of those currently working, and not from income on capital set aside to honour these claims. Wealth is thus transferred from the young and productive members of society to the elderly, a result which leads Hayek to speculate that the burden on the young may in the future become greater than they are willing to bear (288–9, 292 and 295–7).

Hayek gives several reasons why unitary state systems of social security, as they have developed everywhere, pose a critical threat to freedom. First, these programmes are necessarily coercive. They designate government as the monopoly provider of certain services and give administrators broad discretion to distribute benefits to individuals according to what they are thought to deserve. Systems of state medicine transform doctors into paid servants of the state, subject to instruction by authority as to the provision of medical services (288–90, 300). Second, these programmes are at odds with a healthy democracy. This is partly because their very complexity defeats democratic deliberation about them. Neither ordinary citizens nor their elected represent-atives can understand these complex programmes, so they must depend on the judgement of a few experts who strongly favour the principles underlying the programme in question and are disin-clined to question its core principles (288–91). Also, since govern-ment programmes are expected to provide 'adequate' benefits, as determined politically, they are easily exploited by demagogic politicians and self-interested voters (296). Finally, the central bureaucracy that administers social security programmes also controls the flow of information about them. Its power to engage in 'subsidized propaganda' confers on it 'a power over minds' that is akin to that of a totalitarian state (293; cf. 291–4).

Hayek points out that these unitary state systems are facing difficulties everywhere. They have placed on society 'a steadily growing burden from which it will in all probability again and again attempt to extricate itself by inflation.' Even so, these systems, once established, are very difficult to get rid of. Conceiv-ably sickness and unemployment allowances could be trans-formed gradually into systems of true insurance; but in the case of pensions for the aged, the rising generation, having paid for the needs of the preceding one, can always make a claim to support by the next. Any long-term changes will require the public to recon-sider these programmes: '… democracy will have to learn that it must pay for its own follies and that it cannot draw unlimited checks on the future to solve its present problems' (304–5).

Proportional versus progressive taxation

When it comes to governmental efforts to redistribute wealth, Hayek sees the progressive income tax as an even greater threat to freedom than the welfare state's social security policies. Progressive taxation redistributes wealth more efficiently than such policies; without it, the scope of redistribution 'would be very limited.' Moreover, its appeal is broader: 'Redistribution by progressive taxation has come to be almost universally accepted as just.' Whether joined to the welfare state or not, progressive taxation is now 'the chief means of redistributing incomes.' Moreover, it is the main source of democratic irresponsibility and governmental arbitrariness (306–8).

Hayek advocates proportional taxation, which applies a constant rate to everyone. With a progressive system, by contrast, the rate of taxation increases as the amount being taxed increases. The wealthy pay more under both systems, but at an escalating rate under a progressive one. Hayek uses historical evidence to illustrate his claim that there is no limit, in principle, to how high a progressive rate can go. When a progressive income tax was introduced in Prussia in 1891, the upper rate was 4 per cent. In 1910 Great Britain followed suit, as did the USA in 1913, setting the upper rate at '8¼ and 7 percent, respectively. Yet within thirty years these figures had risen to 97½ and 91 percent' (310). This outcome is not surprising to Hayek, since 'all arguments in support of progression can be used to justify any degree of progression' (313).

The case for progressive taxation, as Hayek presents it, rests mainly on four claims, which we may call scientific, political, expedient and moral; and his aim is chiefly to refute these particular claims.

The advocates of progressive taxation hoped to give it scientific respectability by appealing to utility analysis, specifically to the principle that income has a diminishing marginal utility.

Their argument can be put this way: a rising income is satisfying, especially to poor people; but beyond a certain level of need, the satisfaction derived from income diminishes with the addition of each new increment. This means that taxing the wealthy at a high marginal rate will have little effect on their wellbeing, whereas a transfer of wealth will greatly enhance the wellbeing of the poor. Hayek replies only briefly to this argument, since he thinks that the field of utility analysis has abandoned interpersonal comparisons of utilities, and since he doubts that the principle of decreasing marginal utility properly applies to income, broadly understood as 'all the advantages a person derives from the use of his resources' (309).

The political case rests on the idea that progressive taxation is democratic or, more precisely, that it reflects the will of the majority in communities where it has been enacted. Hayek does not object in principle to the majority determining tax policy, so long as it doesn't 'impose a discriminatory tax burden on a minority' or try to determine what an 'appropriate' income would be (322). The problem, in practice, is that groups with the greatest voting strength have used progressive taxation to shift the tax burden to the wealthier classes. The majority, perhaps to gratify its envy, can push tax rates to confiscatory levels. From Hayek's standpoint, this self-interested strategy is both wrong and short sighted. The strategy is wrong, because the majority, instead of applying a general rule, exempts itself from a policy that it applies to others: 'the majority which determines what the total amount of taxation should be must also bear it at the maximum rate' (322). The strategy is short sighted, because inflation gradually brings the middle classes under the higher rates, without raising their real income. Moreover, taxing the rich at a high rate produces much less revenue than is generally recognised. Hayek estimates that British expenditures on subsidies and services are 'financed mainly by the contributions of the middle and upper ranges of the middle class' (313; cf. 311–13, 315).

Progressive taxation is put forward as an expedient or advantageous policy, but Hayek contests this claim on economic grounds. One of his objections to high marginal tax rates is that they impede capital formation, thus slowing economic growth. Potential savers and investors are the ones hit hardest by high marginal tax rates, especially those persons who expend efforts over time or take risks that might yield large gains in a single year. Moreover, high marginal rates reduce the incentive for individuals to increase their earnings within a given tax year and, what is even more harmful, they misdirect resources by diverting people's energies to less useful activities (316–18). To build up a new business or succeed in a new enterprise, individuals must control considerable resources; and acquiring a fortune in a short time period should be seen as 'a legitimate form of remuneration' for this kind of activity. Discouraging individual capital formation restricts competition, inasmuch as it strengthens 'the position of the established corporations against newcomers.' In effect, 'the tax collector' shelters old firms from competition. Also, by preventing 'the dangerous newcomer from accumulating any capital,' progressive taxation 'checks economic progress and makes for rigidity' (320–21; cf. 318–20).

Progressive taxation has sometimes been justified on the basis of capacity to pay, but this argument was superseded by the claim that such a system produces 'a more just distribution of income' (311). Hayek grants that justice is an appropriate standard for weighing tax systems, but argues that steeply progressive ones are themselves unjust. A just system of taxation, as Hayek conceives it, is one that is limited by a principle or rule that applies to everyone. Progressive taxation is not constrained by any such limiting principle. It applies different rules to different people, depending on their degree of wealth; and it has no principled way of deciding who should be taxed and how much. Progressive systems permit a majority 'to impose a discriminatory tax burden on a minority.' By making actual income relative to one's tax rate, they violate 'what is probably the only universally recognized principle of economic justice, that of "equal pay for equal work."' A whole class of persons is practically deprived of the normal incentives because their income is not in line with the rest. None of these progressive measures can be defended on grounds of justice (313–17, 322).

Proportional taxation meets Hayek's standard of justice. It applies the same general rule to everyone, prevents discrimination against the wealthy and, by requiring that political majorities abide by the rules they enact, deters high rates of taxation. Since the principle of proportionality, like that of progressivity, does not itself specify appropriate rates of taxation, Hayek speculates that the maximum admissible rate of direct taxation might reasonably be set 'at that percentage of the total national income which the government takes in taxation.' It should be noted that Hayek does not object to a majority granting 'to an economically weak minority some relief in the form of a proportionately lower taxation.' Also, to compensate for the effects of indirect taxation, he grants that 'some progression in personal income taxation is probably justified' (332–3).

12 STOPPING COERCION IN EMPLOYMENT (CHAPTER 18)

Hayek points out in an earlier chapter that most people today work as employees of large organisations. Some employees are unionised workers; and it is with reference to them that Hayek takes up the problem of coercion in employment. Hayek acknowledges at one point that coercion should 'be treated as equally illegitimate whether employed for or against organization, by the employer or by the employees;' but he is mostly silent about preventing employer coercion, except to recommend contractual arrangements that provide for a grievance procedure and some degree of employee self-government. Generally speaking, Hayek takes the view that workers' interests are best served by encouraging competition among many employers; and it is likely that he would argue that the need to compete for workers is the most effective check on employer coercion. He acknowledges that workers have the right to voluntary agreement among themselves and also the right to 'withhold their services in concert,' but thinks that there are certain employments where the right to strike should be renounced contractually (278, 276–7, 269).

Coercive unionism

Unions employ coercion to gain benefits for their own members, especially higher wages. In fact, 'raising wages by the use of coercion is today the main aim of unions' (275). Having a monopoly of labour is crucial to this aim, for if unions effectively control all the potential workers, employers must bargain with them. Unions thus use coercive means 'to force unwilling workers into membership and to keep non-members out of employment' (268). If governments followed the Rule of Law, they would prevent coercive labour monopolies; but instead they have sanctioned or tolerated hostile picketing in large numbers, closed or union shop contracts, and secondary strikes and boycotts – all techniques that Hayek would prohibit (274–5, 278–9). Unions get away with coercive techniques partly because they wield great political influence and partly because the public mistakenly thinks that union activities benefit the entire working class. Economists can render a public service by correcting this misconception (273–4).

Unions claim to benefit all workers by raising the general level of wages. To refute this claim, Hayek builds on a distinction between real wages and money wages – a distinction that had been important to his business cycle theory and his critique of Keynesian economics. In a 1942 essay he notes that 'real wages' commonly refers to 'the relation between wages as received by the worker and the prices of the commodities on which he spends those wages.' By this definition, which centres on the worker's purchasing power, real wages can increase if the prices of desired commodities go down or decrease if their prices go up. Inflation pushes up money wages but not real wages, since the price of the goods purchased by workers also rises (1948: 252).

Hayek has no doubt that unions can increase workers' money wages, but can they increase real wages for all? Hayek's answer turns on a distinction between 'all the employed' and 'all wishing to work.' By limiting the supply of labour, unions might be able to increase the real wages of their own members and perhaps even those of all the employed; but as a result some workers will be unable to find jobs. As Hayek explains, 'the real wages of all the employed can be raised by union action only at the price of unemployment.' Taking unemployed workers into account, unions 'cannot in the long run increase real wages for all wishing to work above the level that would establish itself in a free market.' Besides distorting the wage structure, the practice of excluding workers from highly paid occupations produces inequalities among workers and amounts to 'the exploitation of the relatively poor by the better-off.' Also, while union activities can increase the real wages of employed workers, empirical evidence shows that real wages 'have often risen much faster when unions were weak than when they were strong.' Hayek concludes that coercive unionism, despite its claim to benefit all workers, serves the interest of a particular group. It increases real wages for organised workers, but pits them against others who 'will find employment only in the less highly paid jobs' or else 'will not be employed at all' (270; cf. 270–71).

An argument heard frequently today is that real wages have steadily lagged behind society's overall productivity gains, so that for workers to receive their just share of the fruits of economic growth, the power of unions to bargain on their behalf must be strengthened. This argument assumes that union practices raise productivity. Hayek undercuts it by insisting that union practices lower productivity, rather than enhancing it. In most European countries, unions employ 'restrictive policies of a "make-work" character' that 'necessarily reduce the productivity of labor all around and therefore also the general level of real wages' (271; cf. 272–3).

Economic and political dangers

Hayek's principled objection to coercive unionism is that it violates the Rule of Law. But he also argues that union wage policy is 'economically very harmful and politically exceedingly dangerous' (272). Some of these economically harmful consequences – distortion of the wage structure, unjustified inequalities among workers, diminished productivity – we have mentioned. Union activities also restrict the mobility of labour, disadvantage some industries more than others, and (often in collusion with enterprise) produce monopolies that limit competition (280–81). But why, besides causing economic harm, are union policies 'exceedingly dangerous' politically? Hayek fears that these policies will lead to a 'system of over-all socialist planning' (273) or 'the transformation of the whole of society into a centrally planned and administered system' (282).

Hayek identifies two distinct but related causes that can produce this dangerous result: the crippling of market allocations; and runaway inflation. The first point is that unions, by establishing monopolies in the supply of labour, 'prevent competition from acting as an effective regulator of the allocation of all resources.' Yet the only alternative to the market as a means of such regulation is 'direction by authority,' which in practice would mean central planning by the state (272–3). Hayek's second point is that steep and prolonged inflation, resulting from an uncontrollable wage–price spiral, will eventually cause serious public alarm and provoke demands 'either for the fixing of wages by government or for the complete abolition of the unions' (282).

Union wage policies cannot alone cause inflation to grow. Excessively high wages would simply produce job losses, if government did not expand the supply of money and credit in order to ensure full employment (see 337). Hayek attributes this ruinous governmental policy to Keynesian economics. Keynes recognised that excessively high wages cause extensive unemployment, but at the same time he saw that any direct attempt to lower wages would require 'a struggle so painful and prolonged that it could not be contemplated.' Keynes's solution was to lower real wages by lowering the value of money: 'If labor insists on a level of money wages too high to allow of full employment, the supply of money must be so increased as to raise prices to a level where the real value of the prevailing money wages is no longer greater than the productivity of the workers seeking employment' (280).

A full employment policy requires the monetary authorities to 'provide enough money to secure full employment at any given wage level.' Such a monetary policy creates expectations of rising inflation. If the money supply is tightened to stop inflation, substantial unemployment will quickly result, bringing about 'a renewed and irresistible pressure for more inflation' (281). Eventually the public, alarmed by spiralling inflation, will demand the drastic actions mentioned above – wage-fixing by government and even the abolition of unions. While opposing the goal of full employment, Hayek does hold that it is possible to secure 'a high and stable level of employment' while aiming at the stability of some comprehensive price level (337).

Hayek is no fatalist. He holds out hope that the dangers he foresees from coercive unionism can be averted. This would require that unions conform to the Rule of Law, which in practice means that government would prevent unions from using coercion to attain their goals. Hayek does not wish to eliminate unions, for this would violate their freedom of association. In fact, he emphasises that unions would continue to have 'a useful and important role,' even with the elimination of their power to coerce individuals. Unions could take part in collective negotiations to settle compensation issues, such as choosing among alternative benefits, setting differences in remuneration for different jobs, and deciding on rules of promotion. Unions could help to determine rules governing the conditions of work, including grievance procedures and some degree of employee self-government. Finally, unions could return to the original model of 'friendly societies,' helping members to protect themselves against the risks of their trade. Unions would be excluded, however, from participating in the conduct of business (276–7). Hayek rests his hopes for reform on the possibility that the public, along with 'farsighted union leaders,' will recognise the dangers inherent in coercive unionism and agree to re-establish the Rule of Law in the workplace (284).

13 PREVENTING INFLATION (CHAPTER 21)

In the mid-1970s, looking back on a long career, Hayek would write that 'the task of preventing inflation has always seemed to me to be of the greatest importance' (2009: 128). Certainly this concern is evident in *The Constitution of Liberty*, which warns repeatedly of inflation's grave consequences. Chapter 21, entitled 'The Monetary Framework', addresses the problem of inflation in three ways: it summarises the inflationary effects of welfare state policies; it demonstrates that monetary policy is central to the problem at hand; and it considers how best to arrange the monetary system so as to prevent inflation. In reading this present chapter, one should keep in mind that Hayek will later reject the monetary arrangement proposed here and embrace a quite different one.

Inflation and the welfare state

Hayek has identified several reasons why welfare state policies are inflationary. Inflation helps to extricate governments from the heavy financial burden of social security programmes, especially old-age pensions. Inflation expands government revenues, under systems of progressive taxation, by moving taxpayers into higher tax brackets, so that their taxable income goes up without a proportional increase in their disposable income. Government's full employment policies, combined with coercive wage pressures by unions, lead to spiralling inflation. Hayek points out that welfare state policies and inflation have a reciprocal relationship, inasmuch as inflation's effects have 'strengthened the demand for welfare measures' (328).

Hayek regards inflation as 'infinitely more dangerous' in the long term than deflation, so the primary goal of monetary policy must be to prevent it. His position runs counter to 'the existing inflationary bias,' which rests on the erroneous belief that deflation is the greater danger (330). Technically speaking, inflation is much easier to prevent than deflation, but psychological and political factors make it difficult to adopt the proper measures. This is because inflation is more pleasant in its immediate effects and deflation more painful. Inflation seems to offer governments an easy way out of deflation, but this is to disregard its long-term disadvantages – a myopic outlook that Keynes sanctioned by the 'fundamentally antiliberal aphorism, "in the long run we are all dead."' To maintain its stimulative effects, even mild inflation must be 'progressively accelerated.' This disrupts business planning, making it more difficult to determine real costs, profits or income. Inflation deters investments by taxing profits more heavily and also erodes savings. Hayek warns again, as he had earlier, that severe inflation can eventually undermine a free society (337–9). For these reasons, 'the economist should always stress the dangers of inflation' (333).

Misguided monetary policy

Besides continually warning against inflation, Hayek pins responsibility for it directly on government: inflation 'is always the result of the weakness or ignorance of those in charge of monetary policy – though the division of responsibility may be spread so wide that nobody is to blame' (295). Much of the present chapter is devoted to ways of maintaining a stable monetary system – one that can reasonably expect to achieve 'a high and stable level of employment' as well as 'the stability of some comprehensive price level' (337).

One option would be to deprive governments of their control over monetary policy and rely on spontaneous market forces to correct inflation and deflation. The market-only option, while perhaps feasible at one time, is no longer practicable or even desirable, and this is for three reasons: first, the need for a central agency to control rapid and disruptive changes in the relative supply of money or the demand for it (money is 'a kind of loose joint in the otherwise self-steering mechanism of the market,' hindering any direct return to a new equilibrium); second, the need to deal with spontaneous fluctuations in the supply of money resulting from 'the interacting money and credit systems;' and third, the need to take account of government's financial policy, which necessarily dominates monetary policy in an era of massive expenditures. It is thus inevitable, under modern conditions, that control of monetary arrangements 'should be largely exercised by governments' (325; cf. 324–7; see Hayek, 1941 [2007a]: 367).

Having argued that the money supply should be controlled by some government agency, Hayek must now decide how much discretion to allow it. One possibility is to impose some mechanical rule that aims for long-term monetary stability but ties the agency's hands in the short term and insulates it from political pressures. Some economists have advocated restrictive rules of this kind. Others would require that currency be convertible into gold or other commodities. Hayek doubts, however, that any of these mechanical solutions were practicable at that time (333–5). Discretion here can be limited, but never eliminated. In fact, central banks require 'much discretion' to fulfil their task of forestalling or counteracting 'developments in the realm of credit, for which no simple rules can provide sufficient guidance.' Additionally, when it comes to preventing great fluctuations in prices and employment, a central bank cannot always wait 'until rule or mechanism forced it to take action' (336).

The denationalisation of money

By the mid-1970s, Hayek had concluded that any central bank that monopolises the issuance of all kinds of money would succumb to political pressures and eventually inflate the currency to dangerous levels. Thus he came to advocate 'the denationalisation of money,' which deprives government of its monopoly of the issue of money and permits banks to offer competing currencies, though not the official one (Hayek, 1978b [2009]). In *The Constitution of Liberty*, Hayek wrestles with the problem of achieving monetary stability even while leaving governmental institutions in control of the money supply. His later strategy, by ending this government monopoly or 'denationalising' money, offers a market-based solution to the problem. Having to compete with other currencies would 'impose a very necessary discipline upon the governmental issue of currency through the threat of its being displaced by a more reliable one.' With citizens free to choose the most trustworthy currency, government would 'be deprived not only of one of the main means of damaging the economy and subjecting individuals to restrictions of their freedom but also of one of the chief causes of its constant expansion.' While severely limiting government's discretion in matters of monetary policy, Hayek does see a need for considerable discretion in its management of financial policy. As 'the biggest spender and investor,' government should, insofar as practicable, 'distribute its expenditure over time in such a manner that it will step in when private investment flags, and thereby employ resources for public investment at the least cost and with the greatest benefit to society' (1979: 59; cf. 57–8).

In view of Hayek's later position, it should be mentioned that in *The Constitution of Liberty* he does question, in a lengthy footnote, whether central banks should monopolise the issue of all kinds of money: 'there seems to be no reason whatever why the state should ever prohibit the use of other kinds of media of exchange, be it some commodity or money issued by another agency, domestic or foreign' (520–21). The footnote does not consider whether competition from private banks might be sufficient to restrain government's monetary institutions.

14 SAFEGUARDING PROGRESS (CHAPTERS 22, 23, 24)

Hayek concludes his discussion of freedom in the welfare state with chapters on housing and town planning, agriculture and natural resources, and education and research. These policy areas, like the ones we examined earlier, involve issues of wealth redistribution, but more broadly they raise questions about progress – what it means, why it is threatened by current policies, and how best to ensure its continuation.

The complex problems of rural and city life and of dwindling natural resources have a common origin in the advance of modern technology. Hayek points out that the Industrial Revolution was preceded and made possible by a revolution in agriculture, which made it possible for a smaller number of farmers to feed the populace. Many rural inhabitants then moved to the cities and took up industrial pursuits, which themselves were highly productive and greatly beneficial to both urban and rural consumers. The decline in the size of the farming population is often lamented on economic and aesthetic grounds; but Hayek sees this decline as a necessary and beneficial adaptation to technological change. As for cities, their growth was determined mostly by undirected market forces and not by advance planning. In Hayek's view, 'the market has, on the whole, guided the evolution of cities more successfully, though imperfectly, than is commonly realized;' and proposals for a system of central direction 'show little awareness of what such a system would have to accomplish, even to equal the market in effectiveness' (342; cf. 358–9, 363, 366, 525, n. 8).

Hayek relies chiefly on markets to ameliorate problems of land use, population imbalances and possible resource depletion. Central planning cannot solve these problems, and it is likely to make them worse. Good policies will facilitate adaptation and help markets work effectively.

Besides considering where progress has brought us, Hayek looks ahead to the requirements for its continuation. Progress is driven above all by new knowledge. Indeed, the emergence and spread of knowledge is a large part of what Hayek means by progress. As we will see, this forward-looking stance is particularly evident in his concluding discussion of education and research policy.

Urban policy

Hayek traces human progress to the growth of cities. Urban life was responsible not only for enormous increases in industrial production and material comforts, but also for advances in science and art. The advantages of civilization over primitive society are due to the city; and since its products can be enjoyed in the country, a leisured life in the country has come to be seen as 'the ideal of a cultured life' in advanced civilisations. Yet despite its indispensable contribution to civilisation and to progress, the city 'is at the same time responsible for the darkest blotches on this civilization.' City life produces a level of poverty and outward signs of squalor that fellow men find shocking and scarcely tolerable (340–41).

Hayek has no objection to planning as a way to deal with

problems of urban life, so long as it is voluntary. The important consideration is whether planning aims 'to supplement and assist the market or to suspend it and put central direction in its place.' By relying on markets, voluntary planning can make 'full use of the dispersed knowledge of the prospects and possibilities of development.' To be sure, the price mechanism is sometimes an imperfect guide, as in determining whether an urban property owner's actions have benefited or harmed his neighbours; but generally it conveys information that is indispensable to voluntary planning (341, 349–50, 352).

Hayek objects to some urban planning measures (rent restrictions, public housing and subsidised housing) because they subject segments of the population to arbitrary decisions and make them dependent on authority for direction in their lives (344). He regards some other measures, such as building regulations and permits, as necessary and desirable, but warns that they are frequently used 'to impose harmful or wholly irrational restrictions on development' and also to 'strengthen the quasi-monopolistic positions of local producers' (355). Controlling land use is one of the principal ways in which urban planners try to channel economic growth. Planners might, for example, specify where industry and commerce can be located or clear away slum housing in the city's centre so as to promote some alternative use of the land.

Hayek does not reject land use planning as such, but recognises that it can make matters worse by preventing evolutionary solutions and by depriving individual owners of an interest in putting their land to better use. In no case should planners expropriate land below fair market value. As for clearing slums, a market solution would be to charge slum properties for the costs they impose on the rest of the city. The slums would probably disappear and be replaced by commercial or industrial buildings. Slum clearance is hard to justify, however, in terms of what is good for the slum dwellers. The poor find it economically advantageous to live in centrally located slums; and public housing is not a desirable option. Subsidising people to remain in the city has the effect of stimulating 'the growth of cities beyond the point where it is economically justifiable.' Moreover, it deliberately creates 'a class dependent on the community for the provision of what they are presumed to need.' A logical next step for planners, in addressing urban problems, would be to control who will be allowed to move into a city. Their inclination, in any event, is to subject the whole economy to 'administrative despotism' (347–8, 351, 354).

Agricultural policy

Agricultural policy in Western countries must face up to the fact that a population's food requirements, even if growing, can be met by fewer farmers than ever before, owing to enormous gains in agricultural productivity. Having too many agricultural workers depresses average farm income and produces rural poverty. Although agriculture is 'peculiarly sluggish in its adaptation to change,' rural workers themselves have gradually dealt with their plight by moving to other jobs, particularly in urban industries. Governments should encourage and facilitate this redistribution of workers by allowing the marginal land and farms to be eliminated. With fewer workers supplying agricultural products, average farm income would rise and might keep up with the general increase in incomes. In fact, however, governments have delayed the necessary adjustment by trying to maintain a much larger agricultural workforce than markets alone would require. The primary tools of this misguided policy are subsidies and controls. Price supports and other farm subsidies amount to 'compulsory transfers of income from the urban to the agricultural population.' More dangerous, in terms of direct coercion, are efforts to control prices and production. Current agricultural policy, to be successful, requires authoritative decisions as to 'who is to produce, how much, and what.' Such a policy leaves little room for individual freedom and leads towards 'a totalitarian control of all economic activity' (362; cf. 360, 361–2).

How might government properly address the genuine and important problems faced by agricultural workers? In Hayek's view, no planning is needed in this area. Generally economic markets should be allowed to take their course. Only the pressure of prices, by producing 'the necessary reduction in the agricultural population' and encouraging the adoption of new agricultural techniques, can 'lower cost and make the survival of the suitable units possible.' Beyond this, there are two specific functions that government ought to perform. First, it should gradually improve legal institutions with a view to making markets work more effectively. Here Hayek takes note of the benefits derived in medieval Europe from the consolidation of dispersed holdings and in England from enclosures of the commons. His point is that legal changes might still be required to bring 'appropriate units of enterprise under single control' and to foster 'group collaboration.' Achieving this result might require 'compulsory expropriation,' but with proper safeguards. Second, government ought to provide a variety of services to agricultural workers, especially informing them about the benefits of technological innovations (see 360, 364–5).

Natural resource policy

The latter half of Chapter 23 addresses indirectly this enduring question: how is humankind to regard 'a free gift of nature'? With some exceptions, Hayek views nature's gifts as an available supply or 'resource' to be used in fostering economic progress. Much government policy, by contrast, is premised on the idea that natural resources have a special standing, such that they must be preserved and protected from exploitation by private enterprise, even with far-reaching controls that greatly limit individual freedom. Hayek replies that a natural resource should be treated the same way as other resources, such as 'man-made equipment or human capacities,' that might be invested in productive activity (367, 373–4).

Hayek points out that some natural resources are diminished by use and are eventually used up, while others can be so managed as to yield a durable stream of benefits. In either case, however, he has no objection to exhausting a natural resource, if that appears to be the best strategy to maximise income. The market offers better foresight in these matters than government planning; and one lesson of advancing technology has been that new and unanticipated resources will emerge to replace existing ones (368–70, 374).

Most of the arguments for 'government control of private activity in the interest of conservation of natural resources' are, in Hayek's view, invalid. He recognises an exception, however, where the aim is not income maximisation, but providing recreational opportunities and preserving natural beauty or sites of historical or scientific interest. Such amenities render a service to the public at large, providing advantages for which the individual beneficiary cannot be charged a price. Also, they usually require large tracts of land. These considerations make the provision of such amenities 'an appropriate field for collective effort.' Voluntary efforts in this field are desirable, but Hayek does not object to government using its compulsory powers to acquire the land needed for such amenities, 'so long as the community approves this, in full awareness of the cost, and realizes that this is one aim competing with others and not a unique objective overriding all other needs' (375; cf. 374–5).

Education and research policy

Hayek's discussion of education is divided roughly into two parts. The first considers education as it might be typified by the elementary school. The second part discusses education as typically provided by the research university, whose aim is not only to disseminate knowledge by instruction, but also to advance knowledge by path-breaking research. The community has an interest in supporting both kinds of education, but for different reasons. Also, both kinds are relevant to progress and to freedom, but in different ways.

While parents have the primary responsibility for the education of their children, the 'other members of the community have a genuine stake' in their welfare. First, the community benefits when knowledge is disseminated widely and used effectively. The spread of useful knowledge increases material opportunities for large numbers of people. Second, if a community is governed by democratic institutions, these are not likely to work well if there is widespread illiteracy. Finally, the community has a stake in 'maintaining certain standards of values,' especially when immigrant populations must be assimilated: 'all education must be and ought to be guided by definite values.' A general education can be an effective way to spread common values and thereby ensure 'a peaceful common existence.' Hayek warns, however, that the attempt to inculcate values is 'the source of real dangers in any system of public education.' A government policy of providing a common cultural background for all citizens 'can lead to frictions in multinational states.' Even in ethnically homogeneous states, there is a danger that government will exert 'a high degree of control of the contents of education' or impose some particular theory of education that claims to be scientific.

General education aims more at preserving civilisation than at novelty. It advances material wealth, but within an established order whose traditions and values it affirms. General education must be compulsory up to a point and government must fund it. This does not mean, however, that general education must be provided in state-run schools. Here the danger of imposing a single set of values or a single theory of education would be great. While the community has an interest in maintaining common values, its overriding interest lies in preserving freedom; and it best achieves this by sponsoring a wide variety of educational arrangements. Hayek points to voucher systems as a way for government to defray the costs of general education without monopolising instruction (378–81).

University education, by contrast, is not intended to conserve established ways or to be immediately useful. The community's interest in supporting university education lies chiefly in the long-term contribution it makes to overall progress or to 'the growth of civilization.' Universities spur progress mainly through the advancement of new knowledge or 'the conception and pursuit of new ideas,' and this 'will always be the work of the relatively few.'

Hayek urges 'that there should be as many independent centers of work as possible,' providing capable and devoted researchers with the freedom to reach and expound their own conclusions, regardless of whether these conclusions 'are palatable to their employer or the public at large' (389–90).

Academic freedom is granted to universities to protect them against outside pressures to affirm the prevailing conventions and values. While approving the doctrine of academic freedom, Hayek warns that conformist pressures often come from within the university. In particular, he opposes 'the ideal of a unified and centralized direction of scientific efforts,' whether directed by outside authorities or by some committee of distinguished scientists (391). The planning of science must inevitably fail to reach its objectives, because the outcome of scientific research is unpredictable. It depends in large degree on accident and on unforeseeable events. No one can say in advance what line of inquiry or what particular researcher will be successful. Hayek expects that individual scientists, making the best use of their opportunities, will more likely succeed in making important discoveries than research teams (392–93; cf. 388–94).

By contrast to elementary schools, research universities can support only a few students at public expense. The community's interest here is not to help particular students, but to advance civilisation. Even so, the recipients of aid have opportunities that are not available to others; and as a result of their superior education, they are likely to enjoy greater wealth and social esteem. Are these state-fostered inequalities justifiable? Here, as in earlier chapters of *The Constitution of Liberty*, Hayek opposes efforts to equalise opportunities, arguing that the public's interest is best served by allowing individuals to make full use of the opportunities available to them, even though these opportunities are limited to a few and inequality is the inevitable outcome (382, 385–6).

Political philosophers traditionally have taught that each political regime aims to produce the type of citizen that accords with that regime; and Hayek agrees that this has been the case. He insists, however, that moulding citizens of a particular type is not the proper business of government. To do so is to presume to know what type of human being the future will prefer; but we cannot know how the future will assess man's moral and aesthetic qualities. The solution is to encourage a variety of types. Freedom means that 'no superior must be allowed to enforce one set of views of what is right or good' and that 'only further experience can decide what should prevail.' Each generation must endeavour to add its share 'in the growth of knowledge and the gradual advance of moral and aesthetic beliefs' (394; cf. 380).

Hayek cautions against expecting too much from general enlightenment. Rationalist liberalism set out to 'conquer ignorance,' but Hayek doubts that such a goal is feasible or that society can be improved this way: 'There is not much reason to believe that, if at any one time the best knowledge which some possess were made available to all, the result would be a much better society' (376–80).

Education, properly understood, views man as a being in progress or as one who 'reaches beyond his present self.' Education thus goes hand in hand with human freedom, whose ultimate aim 'is the enlargement of those capacities in which man surpasses his ancestors.' Freedom does have a purpose or aim, although its consequences are unforeseeable. Hayek concludes in this vein by quoting a well-known passage from Humboldt to the effect that liberty's overriding aim is 'human development in its richest diversity' (394). Education is vital to human development, thus understood. This is why a free society's education policy cannot be merely utilitarian.

15 WHY I AM NOT A CONSERVATIVE (POSTSCRIPT)

When Hayek, in the body of his text, attacks rival views, his targets are mainly rationalist liberalism and socialism in one form or another. To be sure, he sometimes criticises conservative thought and practice; but given his insistence on the limits of reason, the force of tradition and the need to recover old principles, the reader might well conclude that the term 'conservative' applies aptly to Hayek. This notion is exploded by Hayek's Postscript, which repudiates conservatism in no uncertain terms. The Postscript summarises some leading points made in the body of the work, so framed as to highlight Hayek's fundamental disagreement with conservatism. Yet if the Postscript were merely a summary, it would not have become – as it has become – the most widely read and discussed part of *The Constitution of Liberty*. By framing the Postscript as a hard-nosed critique of conservatism, Hayek guaranteed that it would be controversial and would gain a wide audience.

Why did Hayek wish to distance himself from conservatism? By his account, the Conservative Party of Britain and their equivalents in European nations had long resisted free market ideas and favoured expansive government, especially one that would maintain established privileges. The conservative parties, rather than resisting the collectivist tide, had accommodated it: 'It has been regularly the conservatives who have compromised with socialism and stolen its thunder' (398–9). Hayek thus perceived 'true conservatism' to be liberty's adversary rather than its ally. As a defender of liberty, he wanted to draw an indelible line between his position and that of the conservatives.

In the USA there was neither a long-standing conservative party nor a major socialist party. Americans who cherished the original Constitution were not conservatives in Hayek's sense, because they appealed finally to the ideal of liberty that the Constitution embodies. The term 'conservative' came into wide use in the USA after World War II to indicate opposition to 'liberalism,' which in the American context meant chiefly the statist principles and policies of Franklin D. Roosevelt's New Deal. A burgeoning conservative movement emerged in the 1950s, drawing inspiration from diverse thinkers and writers who in one way or another defended individual freedom and limited government. This movement was an uneasy coalition of 'traditionalists' and 'libertarians,' or of humanists who worried about moral or religious decline and proponents of free market economics who wished to curb government's power. Hayek's writings greatly influenced the latter group, and he came to be classified as a libertarian conservative. Hayek did not wish to be identified as a conservative, even in this loose American sense, or as a libertarian.

In the body of the Postscript, Hayek raises specific objections to historical conservatism and shows how it differs from true liberalism. Conservatism lacks principles or goals of its own and thus is unable to offer an alternative to current developments; it seeks to prevent or limit innovation, since it fears change and the impact of new ideas; it is fond of authority and willingly uses it to make individuals conform to acceptable values, goals and moral and religious beliefs; it invokes 'the authority of supernatural sources of knowledge' when reason fails (406); it assigns special privileges to persons whom authority recognises as superior and uses the state to preserve social hierarchy; it distrusts democracy and blames it for present evils; it lacks sufficient knowledge of economics to see that spontaneous forces of adjustment can be counted on to produce beneficial order and growth in the future as they have in the past; and it is stridently nationalistic, even to the point of endorsing imperialistic missions to civilise other peoples.

True liberalism, by contrast, is guided by principles and by a theory of social order; it welcomes change and the generation of new ideas; it invests authority in the law and, because power corrupts, favours the Rule of Law over the rule of men; it is tolerant of moral and cultural diversity and thus makes it possible for persons with different values to coexist peacefully; it acknowledges our inescapable ignorance and avoids explanations that invoke the supernatural; it denies that anyone can say, absent competition, who the superior persons are, and also rejects the notion that such persons should live by different rules, be guaranteed a special position in society, or be sheltered from forces of economic change; it regards democracy as the least evil (and therefore the best practicable) form of government; it is willing to let the market work, since it assumes that in economic matters particularly, 'the self-regulating forces of the market will somehow bring about the required adjustments to new conditions' (400); and its outlook is cosmopolitan rather than nationalistic (399–407).

Hayek identifies himself with what he calls 'the party of liberty' or 'the party of life.' The party of liberty goes back to the eighteenth century, and it does not coincide with any political party or partisan coalition of Hayek's day. Its aim is to promote freedom by influencing opinion, and this it does mainly by formulating ideas that will govern society in the long run. Hayek had worked tirelessly in the 1940s and 1950s for the rebirth of a liberal movement in Europe. In appealing to like-minded scholars, he advised them to stand for 'the highest ideals and keep free from the political disputes of the day.' Devotion to liberal ideals should protect them from the risk 'of becoming involved in party passions.'

The party of liberty was the only kind of party that Hayek, as a political philosopher, could embrace. The political philosopher seeks to shape opinion by defending general principles in an uncompromising way. Party leaders, by contrast, 'organize people for action' – a task that requires them to downplay differences of principle among their followers and to aim for what seems politically possible at the moment (411). The politician lets sleeping dogs lie; the political philosopher stirs controversy. The politician seeks short-term results; the political philosopher understands that far-reaching alterations in institutions or policies are possible only through a change in public opinion. By taking the long view in the 1950s and 1960s and sticking mainly to the philosopher's task of stating or clarifying basic principles, Hayek and like-minded persons would contribute decisively to key developments in the 1970s – the transformation of British conservatism into the party of free enterprise and the ascendancy of a market-oriented conservative movement in the USA.

Hayek is perplexed as to what to call 'the party of liberty.' He has ruled out the name 'conservative.' 'Liberal' is accurate historically, but the term no longer means what it did in England at the turn of the nineteenth century, and its US meaning is the opposite of its true meaning. 'Libertarian' is 'singularly unattractive' to Hayek and for his taste 'carries too much the flavor of a manufactured term and of a substitute' (407–8). Hayek leaves open the question of whether he objects to libertarian thinking as well as to the term itself. This reticence did not deter Hayek's libertarian critics from attacking *The Constitution of Liberty*, both for inadequately limiting state coercion and for condoning expansive government services.

Hayek has racked his brain unsuccessfully to find 'a word which describes the party of life, the party that favors free growth and spontaneous evolution' (408). Taking a cue from the English Whigs, whose ideals inspired liberal movements in the whole of Europe and in the American colonies, he finally concludes that 'Whiggism is historically the correct name for the ideas in which I believe.' By the mid-nineteenth century, Whig parties in both Britain and the USA had been discredited. Nevertheless, Hayek's studies in the evolution of ideas have made him increasingly aware 'that I am simply an unrepentant Old Whig – with the stress on the "old."' Whiggism 'has been the name for the only set of ideals that has consistently opposed all arbitrary power.' Hayek does not know if reviving this name 'is practical politics,' but this is not his main concern as a political philosopher. The 'party of liberty' or 'party of life' that he wants to revive is a broad movement of ideas that may, in the long term, affect political affairs. Making it into a political party would give it an altogether different character (408–10).

BIBLIOGRAPHY

Works of F. A. Hayek

1937 'Economics and knowledge', *Economica*, IV (new ser., 1937), 33–54. Reprinted in Hayek (1948: 33–56).

1941 [2007a] *The Pure Theory of Capital. Collected Works*, vol. 12, ed. Lawrence H. White, Chicago, IL: University of Chicago Press.

1944a 'Historians and the future of Europe'. Reprinted in Hayek (1992: 201–15).

1944b [2007b] *The Road to Serfdom. Collected Works*, vol. 2, Chicago, IL: University of Chicago Press.

1948 *Individualism and Economic Order*, Chicago, IL: University of Chicago Press.

1952a *The Sensory Order*, Chicago, IL: University of Chicago Press.

1952b [1979] *The Counter-Revolution of Science*, Glencoe, IL: Free Press. Second edn: Indianapolis, IN: Liberty Fund.

1954 *Capitalism and the Historians,* ed. with Introduction (pp. 3–29) by Hayek, Chicago, IL: University of Chicago Press.

1955 *The Political Ideal of the Rule of Law*, Cairo: Bank of Egypt.

1960 *The Constitution of Liberty*, Chicago, IL: University of Chicago Press.

1964 'Kinds of order in society', *New Individualist Review*, 3(2) (Winter): 3–12. Reprinted in Hayek (1967). Available at the Online Library of Liberty.

1967 *Studies in Philosophy, Politics, and Economics*, Chicago, IL: University of Chicago Press.

1973 *Rules and Order*, vol. 1 of *Law, Legislation and Liberty*, Chicago, IL: University of Chicago Press.

1976 *The Mirage of Social Justice*, vol. 2 of *Law, Legislation and Liberty*, Chicago, IL: University of Chicago Press.

1978a *New Studies in Philosophy, Politics, Economics, and the History of Ideas*, Chicago, IL: University of Chicago Press.

1978b [2009] *Denationalisation of Money*, London: Institute of Economic Affairs. Reprinted in Hayek (2009: 138–229).

1979 *The Political Order of a Free People*, vol. 3 of *Law, Legislation and Liberty*, Chicago, IL: University of Chicago Press.

1988 *The Fatal Conceit: The Errors of Socialism*, ed. W. W. Bartley III, vol. 1 of *Collected Works*, Chicago, IL: University of Chicago Press.

1992 *The Fortunes of Liberalism*, ed. Peter G. Klein, vol. 4 of *Collected Works*, Chicago, IL: University of Chicago Press and Indianapolis, IN: Liberty Fund.

1994 *Hayek on Hayek: An Autobiographical Dialogue*, ed. Stephen Kresge and Leif Wenar, supplement to *Collected Works*, Chicago, IL: University of Chicago Press and Indianapolis, IN: Liberty Fund.

2009 *Good Money, Part II*, ed. Stephen Kresge, vol. 6 of *Collected Works*, Chicago, IL: University of Chicago Press and Indianapolis, IN: Liberty Fund.

Other works

Locke, John (1690 [1988]) *The Second Treatise of Government*, in Peter Laslett (ed.), *Two Treatises of Government*, Cambridge: Cambridge University Press.

Mill, John Stuart (1975) *On Liberty*, ed. David Spitz, New York: W. W. Norton.

Miller, Eugene F. (1972) 'The cognitive basis of Hayek's political thought', in Robert L. Cunningham (ed.), *Liberty and the Rule of Law*, College Station, TX: Texas A&M University Press.

Nietzsche, Friedrich (1954) *Thus Spoke Zarathustra*, trans. Walter Kaufmann, in W. Kaufmann (ed.), *The Portable Nietzsche*, New York: Viking.

Rousseau, Jean-Jacques (1978) *On the Social Contract*, ed. Roger D. Masters and trans. Judith R. Masters, New York: St Martin's Press.

Schumpeter, Joseph A. (1950) *Capitalism, Socialism and Democracy*, New York: Harper & Row.

Tocqueville, Alexis de (2000) *Democracy in America*, trans. and ed. Harvey C. Mansfield and Delba Winthrop, Chicago, IL: University of Chicago Press.

Weber, Max (1949) *The Methodology of the Social Sciences*, ed. Edward A. Shils, Glencoe, IL: Free Press.

Weber, Max (2004) 'Science as a vocation', in David Owen and Tracy B. Strong (eds), *The Vocation Lectures*, Hackett.

APPENDIX: ANALYTICAL TABLE OF CONTENTS FOR *THE CONSTITUTION OF LIBERTY*

(University of Chicago Press edition, published in the UK by Routledge & Kegan Paul Ltd, paperback 1978)[1]

Introduction

PART I: THE VALUE OF FREEDOM
Chapter 1 Liberty and Liberties

Chapter 2 The Creative Powers of a Free Civilization

---

1   Included by kind permission of the estate of F. A. Hayek and the publishers.

Chapter 3 The Common Sense of Progress

Chapter 4 Freedom, Reason, and Tradition

Chapter 5 Responsibility and freedom

Chapter 6 Equality, Value, and Merit

Chapter 7 Majority Rule

Chapter 10 Law, Commands, and Order

Chapter 11 The Origins of the Rule of Law

Chapter 12 The American Contribution: Constitutionalism

Chapter 13 Liberalism and Administration: The Rechtsstaat

Chapter 14 The Safeguards of Individual Liberty

Chapter 21 The Monetary Framework

Chapter 22 Housing and Town Planning

Chapter 23 Agriculture and Natural Resources

Chapter 24 Education and Research

Postscript: Why I Am Not a Conservative

ABOUT THE IEA

The Institute is a research and educational charity (No. CC 235 351), limited by guarantee. Its mission is to improve understanding of the fundamental institutions of a free society by analysing and expounding the role of markets in solving economic and social problems.

The IEA achieves its mission by:

- a high-quality publishing programme
- conferences, seminars, lectures and other events
- outreach to school and college students
- brokering media introductions and appearances

The IEA, which was established in 1955 by the late Sir Antony Fisher, is an educational charity, not a political organisation. It is independent of any political party or group and does not carry on activities intended to affect support for any political party or candidate in any election or referendum, or at any other time. It is financed by sales of publications, conference fees and voluntary donations.

In addition to its main series of publications the IEA also publishes a quarterly journal, *Economic Affairs*.

The IEA is aided in its work by a distinguished international Academic Advisory Council and an eminent panel of Honorary Fellows. Together with other academics, they review prospective IEA publications, their comments being passed on anonymously to authors. All IEA papers are therefore subject to the same rigorous independent refereeing process as used by leading academic journals.

IEA publications enjoy widespread classroom use and course adoptions in schools and universities. They are also sold throughout the world and often translated/reprinted.

Since 1974 the IEA has helped to create a worldwide network of 100 similar institutions in over 70 countries. They are all independent but share the IEA's mission.

Views expressed in the IEA's publications are those of the authors, not those of the Institute (which has no corporate view), its Managing Trustees, Academic Advisory Council members or senior staff.

Members of the Institute's Academic Advisory Council, Honorary Fellows, Trustees and Staff are listed on the following page.

The Institute gratefully acknowledges financial support for its publications programme and other work from a generous benefaction by the late Alec and Beryl Warren.

The Institute of Economic Affairs
2 Lord North Street, Westminster, London SW1P 3LB
Tel: 020 7799 8900
Fax: 020 7799 2137
Email: iea@iea.org.uk
Internet: iea.org.uk

Other papers recently published by the IEA include:

Towards a Liberal Utopia?
Edited by Philip Booth
Hobart Paperback 32; ISBN 0 255 36563 2; £15.00

The Way Out of the Pensions Quagmire
Philip Booth & Deborah Cooper
Research Monograph 60; ISBN 0 255 36517 9; £12.50

Black Wednesday
A Re-examination of Britain's Experience in the Exchange Rate Mechanism
Alan Budd
Occasional Paper 135; ISBN 0 255 36566 7; £7.50

Crime: Economic Incentives and Social Networks
Paul Ormerod
Hobart Paper 151; ISBN 0 255 36554 3; £10.00

The Road to Serfdom *with* **The Intellectuals and Socialism**
Friedrich A. Hayek
Occasional Paper 136; ISBN 0 255 36576 4; £10.00

Money and Asset Prices in Boom and Bust
Tim Congdon
Hobart Paper 152; ISBN 0 255 36570 5; £10.00

The Dangers of Bus Re-regulation
and Other Perspectives on Markets in Transport
John Hibbs et al.
Occasional Paper 137; ISBN 0 255 36572 1; £10.00

The New Rural Economy
Change, Dynamism and Government Policy
Berkeley Hill et al.
Occasional Paper 138; ISBN 0 255 36546 2; £15.00

The Benefits of Tax Competition
Richard Teather
Hobart Paper 153; ISBN 0 255 36569 1; £12.50

Wheels of Fortune
Self-funding Infrastructure and the Free Market Case for a Land Tax
Fred Harrison
Hobart Paper 154; ISBN 0 255 36589 6; £12.50

Were 364 Economists All Wrong?
Edited by Philip Booth
Readings 60; ISBN 978 0 255 36588 8; £10.00

Europe After the 'No' Votes
Mapping a New Economic Path
Patrick A. Messerlin
Occasional Paper 139; ISBN 978 0 255 36580 2; £10.00

The Railways, the Market and the Government
John Hibbs et al.
Readings 61; ISBN 978 0 255 36567 3; £12.50

Corruption: The World's Big C
Cases, Causes, Consequences, Cures
Ian Senior
Research Monograph 61; ISBN 978 0 255 36571 0; £12.50

Choice and the End of Social Housing
Peter King
Hobart Paper 155; ISBN 978 0 255 36568 0; £10.00

Sir Humphrey's Legacy
Facing Up to the Cost of Public Sector Pensions
Neil Record
Hobart Paper 156; ISBN 978 0 255 36578 9; £10.00

The Economics of Law
Cento Veljanovski
Second edition
Hobart Paper 157; ISBN 978 0 255 36561 1; £12.50

Living with Leviathan
Public Spending, Taxes and Economic Performance
David B. Smith
Hobart Paper 158; ISBN 978 0 255 36579 6; £12.50

The Vote Motive
Gordon Tullock
New edition
Hobart Paperback 33; ISBN 978 0 255 36577 2; £10.00

Waging the War of Ideas
John Blundell
Third edition
Occasional Paper 131; ISBN 978 0 255 36606 9; £12.50

The War Between the State and the Family
How Government Divides and Impoverishes
Patricia Morgan
Hobart Paper 159; ISBN 978 0 255 36596 3; £10.00

Capitalism – A Condensed Version
Arthur Seldon
Occasional Paper 140; ISBN 978 0 255 36598 7; £7.50

Catholic Social Teaching and the Market Economy
Edited by Philip Booth
Hobart Paperback 34; ISBN 978 0 255 36581 9; £15.00

Adam Smith – A Primer
Eamonn Butler
Occasional Paper 141; ISBN 978 0 255 36608 3; £7.50

Happiness, Economics and Public Policy
Helen Johns & Paul Ormerod
Research Monograph 62; ISBN 978 0 255 36600 7; £10.00

They Meant Well
Government Project Disasters
D. R. Myddelton
Hobart Paper 160; ISBN 978 0 255 36601 4; £12.50

Rescuing Social Capital from Social Democracy
John Meadowcroft & Mark Pennington
Hobart Paper 161; ISBN 978 0 255 36592 5; £10.00

Paths to Property
Approaches to Institutional Change in International Development
Karol Boudreaux & Paul Dragos Aligica
Hobart Paper 162; ISBN 978 0 255 36582 6; £10.00

Prohibitions
Edited by John Meadowcroft
Hobart Paperback 35; ISBN 978 0 255 36585 7; £15.00

Trade Policy, New Century
The WTO, FTAs and Asia Rising
Razeen Sally
Hobart Paper 163; ISBN 978 0 255 36544 4; £12.50

Sixty Years On – Who Cares for the NHS?
Helen Evans
Research Monograph 63; ISBN 978 0 255 36611 3; £10.00

Taming Leviathan
Waging the War of Ideas Around the World
Edited by Colleen Dyble
Occasional Paper 142; ISBN 978 0 255 36607 6; £12.50

The Legal Foundations of Free Markets
Edited by Stephen F. Copp
Hobart Paperback 36; ISBN 978 0 255 36591 8; £15.00

Climate Change Policy: Challenging the Activists
Edited by Colin Robinson
Readings 62; ISBN 978 0 255 36595 6; £10.00

Should We Mind the Gap?
Gender Pay Differentials and Public Policy
J. R. Shackleton
Hobart Paper 164; ISBN 978 0 255 36604 5; £10.00

Pension Provision: Government Failure Around the World
Edited by Philip Booth et al.
Readings 63; ISBN 978 0 255 36602 1; £15.00

New Europe's Old Regions
Piotr Zientara
Hobart Paper 165; ISBN 978 0 255 36617 5; £12.50

Central Banking in a Free Society
Tim Congdon
Hobart Paper 166; ISBN 978 0 255 36623 6; £12.50

Verdict on the Crash: Causes and Policy Implications
Edited by Philip Booth
Hobart Paperback 37; ISBN 978 0 255 36635 9; £12.50

The European Institutions as an Interest Group
The Dynamics of Ever-Closer Union
Roland Vaubel
Hobart Paper 167; ISBN 978 0 255 36634 2; £10.00

An Adult Approach to Education
Alison Wolf
Hobart Paper 168; ISBN 978 0 255 36586 4; £10.00

Taxation and Red Tape
The Cost to British Business of Complying with the UK Tax System
Francis Chittenden, Hilary Foster & Brian Sloan
Research Monograph 64; ISBN 978 0 255 36612 0; £12.50

Ludwig von Mises – A Primer
Eamonn Butler
Occasional Paper 143; ISBN 978 0 255 36629 8; £7.50

Does Britain Need a Financial Regulator?
Statutory Regulation, Private Regulation and Financial Markets
Terry Arthur & Philip Booth
Hobart Paper 169; ISBN 978 0 255 36593 2; £12.50

Other IEA publications

Comprehensive information on other publications and the wider work of the IEA can be found at www.iea.org.uk. To order any publication please see below.

Personal customers

Orders from personal customers should be directed to the IEA:
Sam Collins
IEA
2 Lord North Street
FREEPOST LON10168
London SW1P 3YZ
Tel: 020 7799 8907. Fax: 020 7799 2137
Email: scollins@iea.org.uk

Trade customers

All orders from the book trade should be directed to the IEA's distributor:
Gazelle Book Services Ltd (IEA Orders)
FREEPOST RLYS-EAHU-YSCZ
White Cross Mills
Hightown
Lancaster LA1 4XS
Tel: 01524 68765. Fax: 01524 53232
Email: sales@gazellebooks.co.uk

IEA subscriptions

The IEA also offers a subscription service to its publications. For a single annual payment (currently £42.00 in the UK), subscribers receive every monograph the IEA publishes. For more information please contact:
Sam Collins
Subscriptions
IEA
2 Lord North Street
FREEPOST LON10168
London SW1P 3YZ
Tel: 020 7799 8907. Fax: 020 7799 2137
Email: scollins@iea.org.uk